BIGGER

essays

BIG

REN CEDA

WINNER OF THE 2024 AUTUMN HOUSE NONFICTION PRIZE

GER

ESSAYS

R FULLER

Pittsburgh, PA

Bigger: Essays

Published by Autumn House Press

ISBN: 978-1-63768-108-4

Cover and Book Design by Joel W. Coggins
Author Photo by Deema Almunajem

Cataloging-in-Publication Data for this title is available from the Library of Congress.

Printed in the United States on acid-free paper that meets the international standards of permanent books intended for purchase by libraries.

This book is nonfiction. It reflects the author's present recollections of experiences over time. Some names and characteristics have been changed, some events have been compressed, and some dialogue has been recreated.

Autumn House Press is a nonprofit corporation whose mission is the publication and promotion of poetry and other fine literature. The press gratefully acknowledges support from individual donors, public and private foundations, and government agencies. This book was supported, in part, by the Greater Pittsburgh Arts Council and the Pennsylvania Council on the Arts, a state agency funded by the Commonwealth of Pennsylvania.

CONTENTS

FOR MY LITTLE FAMILY

BIGGER

essays

NAMING MY FATHER

My father could look at a loose metal bolt and say if it was a three-eighths or a five-sixteenths, but he could not name his four daughters unless we were lined up by height. He taught my sisters and me to eat corn on the cob left to right, two even rows at a time, like little typewriters. He walked without bobbing his head up and down, as though it were tied to an overhead cable. When my mother asked my father if he remembered her friend Marjorie, he asked, "The one with symmetrical moles?"

When I was young, I did not know my father was unusual: Our parents show us how people are supposed to be. By the time my sisters and I started to name the things that made our father different, we were grown, and he was gone.

In the 1940s, gator farms in Louisiana shipped live baby alligators through the mail, a dollar and a half for an eight-inch specimen. My grandparents had one shipped to Los Angeles and gave it to my father for his tenth birthday. He named it Al.

"That alligator was your daddy's best friend," said my grandma Leela.

Baby alligators walk with their heads raised up, high-stepping their feet and slapping them flat on the ground. In a black-and-white photo, my ten-year-old father wears his hair slicked back. He is crawling behind Al, both of them with heads held high and legs raised up for the next step.

"He would follow that alligator around for hours," Grandma Leela said. "I don't know why he didn't play with other children."

In 1944, the same year my father got his baby alligator, Dr. Hans Asperger presented a paper in Vienna about a personality difference he called autism. Asperger described his young patients as "socially unconcerned." He noted their extreme reactions if something unexpected happened, but he also described their fascinations with negative numbers, poetry, and spaceships. He said one boy had "rich experiences and his own independent interests . . . one could really learn from him."

People with autism, Asperger wrote, "can fulfill their social role within the community, especially if they find understanding, love and guidance." His paper was written in German and would not be read by American doctors for almost forty years.

The year before Asperger's paper was published, Dr. Leo Kanner at Johns Hopkins had published his own paper about autism. He said the children he studied valued people the way they did "the desk, the bookshelf, or the filing cabinet." They were obsessed with "the maintenance of sameness."

Because he published his paper before Asperger, and in English, Kanner became known in the United States as the father of autism, and his views about autistic children molded American medical practice. Desperate parents took pilgrimages to his clinic and laid their hopes on his desk.

"In the whole group, there are very few really warmhearted

fathers and mothers," Kanner wrote. He coined the term "refrigerator mother."

Believing parents were to blame for autism, Kanner supported parentectomies: sending children with autism to institutions and forbidding visits from their families. He believed the treatment would be infrequent because autism was rare: By the end of his decades-long career, Kanner reported he had seen only 150 cases.

My father graduated from high school in the early 1950s, at the start of the Korean War, and was drafted into the Army. He walked with flat feet, so the Army made him a typist.

Twenty years later, in a dinner-table monologue directed at my sisters and me, our father described having to type with no errors.

"If you made a mistake on a form, even if it was the very last letter of the very last word, you had to type it again," he said. He was smiling.

We sat beneath the world map tacked to the wall, the one he quizzed us on when he wasn't giving a lecture. Not just the continents, countries, and capitals. He quizzed us on the colors, too. "Name the purple countries."

But that night, he lectured about military rules: how to clean a rifle, how to shine your shoes. While my mother and sisters focused on their plates, I mixed my broccoli with potatoes to soften the bitterness and watched my father's shoulders relax while he reminisced about the Army's bounty of rules.

A few years later, I found two shoeboxes in the garage and carried them into the house. They were filled with index cards. My mother and I opened the first box and found cards full of information about military vehicles and weaponry.

“I haven’t seen these in years,” she said. “Your father typed them while he was in the Army.”

Each card listed a piece of equipment, followed by lines of description and a row of reference numbers typed across the bottom. My father had devised a system that let him sort equipment by the manufacturer, the date it was first used by the Army, and a dozen other categories.

In the late 1950s, the G.I. Bill sent my father first to college, where he discovered accounting, and then to grad school to become a C.P.A. He took a job in San Diego and joined a church with a large singles group.

No longer cataloging military equipment for fun, he started typing Bible verses onto index cards; that’s what was in the second shoebox. These, too, had a reference system—lines of numbers and letters across the bottom of each card. My father listed each verse’s sentence type: question, exclamation, command. He cross-referenced hundreds of topics. He noted the speakers. (G. meant God.)

Meanwhile, the American medical establishment continued to follow Leo Kanner’s lead, viewing autism as a behavior issue to be controlled. In addition to parentectomies, over the next few decades, therapists began prescribing tranquilizers, like Thorazine, and hallucinogens, like LSD. Teachers tied children to chairs, slapped their hands, forced them to smell repugnant odors, and withheld food. Shock therapy was common; teachers, parents, and therapists attached electrodes to children’s skin and gave them painful zaps if they did something the adult did not like. If they flapped their hands: zap. If they didn’t look the teacher in the eye: zap.

My parents met in the church singles group in San Diego and married a few months later.

"I was a spinster," my mother explained. She was twenty-six.

She had four babies in six years, in between packing and moving and setting up a new home each time my father left another less-than-perfect job. By the time I was ten, we had moved a dozen times, up and down the state of California.

While our father was at work, my sisters and I were free to play loud games and be rambunctious. At one house, we climbed lemon trees; at another, we made a giant mudhole. Our mother enjoyed our wildness and emotion, until it got to be too much, and then she swatted us.

I don't know if my mother recognized her husband's behavior as odd. She must have known that noise and movement set him off, yet in the evening when we heard his footsteps clomping up the pathway to our house, I sometimes saw her walk over to the stereo and turn the volume up.

My mother did not talk about our father's differences. She seemed as unenlightened as her daughters about how fathers should behave: From the age of seven, she had lived year-round at a boarding school and saw her parents for only two weeks every summer. Still, it would have helped my sisters and me if she had named our father's strangeness and interpreted his actions.

It is easy to blame the mother.

By the time I was in kindergarten, I knew that if I were quiet and made no sudden movements, I could be my father's little helper. When he made ice cream one summer afternoon, he let me hold the ruler inside the wooden bucket while he added the layers of rock salt and crushed ice. He patted each layer flat, then measured it. An ice layer, he insisted, had to be exactly half an inch.

"Don't breathe on the ice," he told me, even though it was already melting from the rock salt and the sunny California day. I turned my head away, careful to hold the ruler straight.

His explosions were instantaneous, yet not unexpected. As ordinary as breakfast cereal. He would yell, kick toys, throw the cat, spank, and scream exaggerations. ("You took three hundred pieces of Kleenex!" he said once, when my sister used two tissues to blow her nose.)

Other things that could make him explode: leaving a game on the floor where he would walk A-to-B across the room. Laughing at dinner if he didn't know why. Eating an apple wrong. Not using the color cup assigned to you at the dinner table. Being ordinary children who would dillydally, zigzag, hoot and holler, bebop.

Now, I understand my father could not appreciate the randomness of children. We didn't lie where he left us like a hammer or a book.

Our father had us memorize the names of the books in the Bible forward, backward, and alphabetically. One Sunday morning in December, when my baby sister, Greta, was in kindergarten and I was in fifth grade, the pastor said our father had a surprise for the congregation. Greta followed our father up the two steps onto the stage of the church.

"C," called our father.

"First and Second Chronicles, First and Second Corinthians, Colossians," Greta said.

"H," said our father. He smiled while Greta called out the books.

He's spelling Christmas, I thought. Adults around me shifted in the pews, and I knew they didn't understand what was happening. *He should have told them what Greta would be spelling,* I thought, and that's when I realized that I could predict how others would feel, and my father could not.

By the time I was in middle school, I had decided my father wasn't normal.

"He can't tell me apart from my sisters," I told my friend Linda while we stood on a street corner, eating corn dogs from the gas station. We were in eighth grade and wore our long blonde hair in braids to minimize the catcalls while we rode our bikes around town.

"Yeah, your dad thought I was one of you," Linda said. "He goes, 'You, Thora, Ren, I mean, Sigrid, hold the pliers.'"

"When?"

"Like, a month ago. I was getting my bike out of your garage."

"What did you do?"

"I held the pliers."

One night, while I peeled the carrots, I asked my mother, "Does he love us?"

"Of course your father loves you."

I kept peeling and thought, *this is what it feels like to have my father love me. It feels like he does not.*

Despite his strangeness, I wanted a connection. Since he did not talk to my sisters or me except to lecture or to quiz, I asked my mother if I could have lunch with him, and she arranged it. She told me to take the bus to Cattlemen's Restaurant on State Street. I dressed up, thirteen years old and gawky, wanting to be pretty. I thought my father would ask about my friends, and I would ask what he liked about accounting. I had seen a father on TV hug his daughter and say, "I'm so proud of you, honey."

Instead, my father talked, with points and subpoints, about the causes of the first World War. I listened and ate my barbecue sandwich.

"What was it like?" Sigrid asked after I arrived home from the bus stop. Greta sat next to her on my bed while I hung up my plastic bead necklace.

"He said I could order anything I wanted, and he talked to me the whole time."

Even though I had failed, I wanted them to feel loved by our father.

In high school, I signed up for an internship at Greta's elementary school. I spent a few weeks each in a kindergarten, in my baby sister's sixth-grade class, and in a special education room for children who met Leo Kanner's criteria for autism.

The special ed class had four children and two teachers. One of the teachers wore a thick rubber band as a bracelet. A seven-year-old boy in the class, whose black hair stuck up every which way, would squawk when he was happy.

"Stop that," said the teacher with the rubber band. She walked over to the boy, took off her bracelet, and snapped it against his bare arm.

The children in the classroom played separately. One liked the color red, another enjoyed things with holes, and one of them loved helicopters. They seemed happy if I followed their familiar routines, but the girl who loved helicopters screamed when I put her water cup too far from her plate.

One of the students had face blindness and did not recognize his mother. Two of them could speak, although they did not answer questions from me like, "Whatcha doing?" The three of them who had physical tics, like squawking or hand flapping, received most of the snaps from the rubber band.

Back then, I did not know any children who were not smacked by their parents, and the teacher's rubber band snapping did not feel abusive to me. Instead, it made me curious. Was there a way to connect with someone who seemed to exist in a different world?

The children in the autism classroom did not remind me of my father. He didn't squawk or have a label, and he was the one who gave punishments, not the one who received them.

My best friend in high school liked my father, and I liked hers. Diane's father made bad jokes and put his arm around my shoulders. He asked about my classes and my job at McDonald's.

"Your dad's a blast," I told Diane.

"No way. Your dad is better. He never bothers us. My dad's an asshole," she said, and I thought, *maybe that's all it is. Maybe fathers are just different kinds of assholes.*

In college, I spent an autumn weekend with my roommate's family in Northern California. On Saturday, Kris and I helped her father rake leaves, and soon the two of them were play-fighting, laughing, stuffing leaves down the backs of each other's shirts. I held my breath: They were playing like my sisters and I played when our father wasn't home. Other fathers enjoy their children, I allowed myself to realize.

I had squeezed down that knowledge for many years. My father did not love me the way he loved his index cards, his ledger sheets, or sorting bolts by sizes. I had wanted to believe that someday I would do things so perfectly he would look at me the way my roommate's father looked at her, but now I saw he never would. Back at our college apartment, after Kris was asleep, I looked out at the dark parking lot and cried into the living room curtains.

Finally, after Greta left for college, our mother left our father.

"I'm sure you have questions," she said on the phone.

"Only why you stayed so long."

"Children need a father in the home."

My mother was crying, so I did not argue. But I felt angry. How could she think his lack of interest in us had been good for my sisters and me?

Leo Kanner's methods remained standard protocol for working with children who were diagnosed with autism into the 1980s. Studies from that decade, however, estimated up to one out of two thousand children had autism—too many to give all of them parentectomies. (In 2024, the CDC reported that one out of thirty-six children in the US is on the autism spectrum.)

By the late 1980s, I was out of college and working in San Francisco. Anger-sadness about my father filled my bus rides through the city, and I joined a therapy group called Rotten Childhoods. After half a year of therapy and no longer feeling bruised, I wondered if I could build a relationship with my father. Maybe he was waiting for me.

I wrote him a letter. Within a week, he wrote back: three pages, typed, single-spaced. He detailed his work history, his fascination with computers, and his innocence in the face of my mother's frustration.

He said, "My feelings about you are positive." I rubbed my fingers across the proof of that line and translated his words to "I love you."

I wrote my father back and invited him to visit me in San Francisco. A month later, he drove up and met me for dinner at Fisherman's Wharf.

"Do you like oysters?" he asked.

"I've never had one."

He ordered a dozen and taught me how to slurp them salty-wet from their shells. He gave me a history lesson about San Francisco and said he didn't know why my mother had left him.

"She's the one who kept me from you girls. She's the one who made our family miserable."

"Let's not talk about Mom," I told my father. I hoped he would ask about me, but he did not.

My father drove up a few more times and met me at Fisherman's Wharf, but I felt more distant with each of his visits. I wished he would stick to writing letters, where I could dig through the typing to find the few words that I needed to hear. My small efforts to see him, though, seemed to tell him we were close.

"I know your sisters take your mother's side," he said while we walked along PIER 39 one afternoon. "But you are on my side." He lifted his feet high over the wooden planks.

My sisters and I did side with our mother. Around that time, I made a list of the ten worst things my mother had done (one, she's so passive; two, she's always crying). But her failings were small compared to the way she smoothed my hair or stayed up past midnight if I needed to talk.

After one of my father's visits, I set a boundary as I'd been taught in therapy.

"I want to have a relationship with you," I wrote, "but I can't listen to you say negative things about Mom." If he wanted me in his life, he had to stop. "When you're ready, I am here. I love you," I said.

I felt guilty about demanding that he change. I was raised to honor thy father.

A week passed. A month. A year of checking the mailbox. I wondered if I should write another letter, but I was new to placing boundaries and held tight to the one I had set.

By the second year, the mailbox no longer felt like a zap each time I found it empty. Day by day, I let go of struggling to understand my father, and it felt like drinking a cold glass of water on a hot California day.

The next year, I moved to Los Angeles for grad school and discovered that substitute teaching on an emergency credential paid more than my research assistant position. I taught a special education class where my nine students, part-time aide, and I were segregated in a portable on the far side of the recess yard.

A few years earlier, the state of California had outlawed corporal punishment in schools, but my principal said, "You can hit them if you need to." I didn't know how to manage a classroom, but I refused to hit my students. Instead, I bribed them with cake.

I hadn't seen my father for several years when Greta invited him to her wedding. Thora, Sigrid, and I called each other before the event. How would we insulate our baby sister if our father unraveled? We designed hand signals to show which of us was closest to Greta, where our father was, and if he seemed calm.

I spotted him from our lineup of sisters at the front of the church. His hair was slicked back, the same way he wore it in that childhood photo with the baby alligator. He seemed composed even though my sisters and I stood in the wrong order—youngest, oldest, middle, middle. During the reception, our father sat quietly at the back, and after a while, Thora, Sigrid, and I ceased our frantic signaling.

Toward the end of the reception, Sigrid asked, "Do you want to go see him?"

I nodded, and we clasped each other's hands and walked across the dance floor.

"Hi, Dad," I said at the same time as Sigrid.

He stared straight ahead, then turned his chair away from us. It squawked on the linoleum floor.

I had imagined, while crossing the dance floor, that he would be happy to see me. By my mid-twenties, I was familiar with the way relationships can move apart and reconnect, and if he had simply stared at Sigrid and me, it would have felt familiar. I would have seen it as an opening. But when my father turned his chair, it severed us.

Now I am a mother, and if my child turned the chair a thousand times, I would keep crossing the dance floor. With my father, I accepted the back of his chair.

Two years after Greta's wedding, Hans Asperger's paper was translated into English. His positive view of people with autism electrified doctors and parents. Within a few years, Asperger's syndrome became the diagnosis for people who had autistic traits yet no cognitive impairment.

When the World Wide Web went public, adults with Asperger's found each other online. They called themselves Aspies. The internet was a swinging vine that let people with autism connect without having to worry about traditional manners or eye contact.

I was a public-school teacher during the years when Aspies discovered each other. One year, I taught fifth grade in a small town in Oregon where the school district wanted to start mainstreaming—moving special education students into regular classrooms. I volunteered my class, and a ten-year-old on the autism spectrum soon joined us, along with his aide. Joey used a picture board to communicate, hooted when he was excited, and was fascinated by wheels.

At the end of the year, I wrote an article for the district newsletter about our mainstreaming success: how Joey sat with us during our class meetings on the rug, how the students took his hand and led him out to recess.

I did not write about the challenges. When Joey saw a car drive past our classroom, he ran to the window to stare at the wheels, and if his aide or I did not stop him, he merrily stripped off his clothes. His aide worked on Joey's communication with a buzz of narration: "Look, Ms. Cedar is writing on the whiteboard." Some days, his aide was absent, and I would hold Joey on my lap, cuddly and wiggly, while teaching the rest of the students.

But I enjoy a lively class, and from then on, I had multi-ability rooms. Teacher training for mainstreaming was high on hope and low on practicality. The trainers wanted us to use sticker sheets as bribes. They said we needed to grab the children's faces to make them look at us, but I do not grab people's faces. Instead, I cleared paths through the classroom for Marco, who needed to walk in straight lines, and I let Laura turn full-body circles in the back of the room.

With my regular-education students, I could tell when they connected with an activity or a new friend. With my children on the spectrum, I never understood how to help them grow, only how to help them not explode.

In 1998, I got married. I did not invite my father to my wedding.

"It's easier to not have him here," one of my sisters whispered to me while we hugged between songs on the dance floor.

My father never met my child. I didn't trust him to stay calm if my baby cried or my toddler romped across the room. I rarely thought about my father in those years, and if someone asked about him, I could tell stories without feeling angry or sad.

One afternoon when my child was two, my mother left a message on the answering machine: "Your father had a heart attack." He died alone.

I waited for a sadness that did not arrive and wondered if grieving through my teens and twenties had satiated me. I thought, *what a loss for him to not enjoy me or my sisters.* I pondered an absence that would now last forever.

When he died alone, did my father believe no one wanted to love him?

After my child started school, I opened a preschool in Bellevue, Washington. It was the land of Microsoft, and some of my little ones' parents were software engineers. One year, a dad told me he was an Aspie.

After drop-off one morning, we stood in the breezeway and

talked about how he never felt like he fit in when he was a child. Now, at Microsoft, he felt like his differences were valued.

At one point, he told me, "I get distracted by your hands." I am a whole-body talker, so I clasped my hands behind my back and tried to stand still.

That night, I repeated the conversation to my husband, Jason, who had also worked in tech. Jason remembered a story in *Wired* magazine called "The Geek Syndrome" and found a copy for me. The author, Steve Silberman, wrote the article in 2001, the year my father died.

"Clumsy and easily overwhelmed in the physical world," Silberman wrote, "autistic minds soar in the virtual realms of mathematics, symbols, and code."

His words allowed me to wonder: What if my father was on the autism spectrum? It was like the maps of the world I used to show my fifth graders with the Southern Hemisphere on top or centering the continent of Africa. "Let's think about the world in a different way."

═══

I called my sisters to share my new theory. For Thora and Greta, the idea was new, but Sigrid said, "Of course he was autistic." That was a decade ago. Today, we all use the label for our father. With a shrug. Probably.

I did not ask my mother. She had squeezed her anger silent while married to my father, and now that he was gone, she had let the bitter loose. Sometimes, to calm her, I would say "Camellia." Her favorite flower, and our code word for *stop, I don't want to hear any more about how terrible he was.*

═══

My diagnosis could be wrong, like when I see an idea in a poem that is not what the poet intended. Even so, believing my father was on the spectrum feels hopeful, like blowing dandelions. If he was on the autism spectrum, it means he may have loved me but was not able to show it, not the way other fathers do.

I am glad my father was not diagnosed with autism when he was a child, that he was not taken from his parents, and did not have electrodes taped onto his skin. Yet I wish his only friend when he was young had not been Al, the baby alligator. And I wish my father had learned how to explain what he needed, like the preschool dad who told me to stop waving my hands.

"You girls look alike to me," our father could have said when my sisters and I were young. "Please name yourself, unless all four of you are lined up in birth order."

I would have given him my name every time I saw him. I would have realized that before he drove up to San Francisco, he must have researched facts about the city as a way of connecting with me. I would have grown up confident he loved me—because he must have. He wanted me to know all the countries in the world, all the stories in his Bible, all the histories he could share. He wanted my world to be bigger, which is what we want for those we love.

EYE CONTACT

In Army flight training, just before World War II, an American we will call Joe flew into a cloud, and when he emerged, his plane was upside down. Questioned later by the flight instructor about why he rotated the plane, Joe didn't have an answer. He thought he was right side up until he flew out of the cloud and saw the ground above him.

The United States needed to train thousands of pilots. Unfortunately, Joe was not the only one to zoom upside down out of a cloud. It didn't make sense: All of the candidates (each of whom was white and male) had top scores on intelligence tests, classroom work, and simulators. Some of them, however, could not tell up from down if a cloud obscured their view.

I didn't realize my left eye was legally blind until the dean of optometry told me. I was at Pacific University's free vision clinic on a Saturday morning in October.

"I wonder why your eyeball isn't flopping around," the dean said.

He wore jeans and a college sweatshirt. "You move it like it is functional."

I knew my eye didn't see well but thought it only affected my depth perception. When people said, "Here, catch," and threw me a set of keys, I looked away. When the keys hit the floor, I would say, "Oops," and pretend I hadn't been paying attention.

I was at the free clinic because I'd moved to Oregon a month before and the Hillsboro DMV used electronic binoculars instead of the paper eye charts used in California. Each of my eyeballs stared into a different lens, and my right eye saw the sailboat, star, and heart, but my left eye saw a blank white rectangle.

"There's nothing on the screen," I told the DMV clerk.

"Sure there is, hon. Look again."

"Am I supposed to see something? There's a light but no picture."

The clerk pushed herself out of her chair and walked around the counter to my side. Her shoes squeaked on the linoleum, and I moved out of the way so she could look through the binoculars.

"Yeah, there's stuff in there," she said.

I looked again and told her I only saw white light.

"Well, your right eye is fine." The clerk motioned me to the photo station.

The blank white screen alarmed me. I had started a new teaching job, and my vision insurance wouldn't kick in for a few months. One of my roommates was a student at the university and told me about the optometry department's free clinic.

That Saturday morning, graduate students who wore crisp white coats bumped me up the row of exam chairs, from a first-year master's student to a second-year, from a doctoral student to the dean. Each optometrist-to-be pointed to an eye chart they'd taped to the wall of the university gym. Sometimes while I held the antiseptic-smelling plastic shield over my right eye, my left eye would slip into focus long enough to read a single letter before sliding back to blurry.

"Good," the graduate students would say when I named a letter correctly.

My final stop, the dean's exam area, was surrounded by a curtain in the corner of the gym. Robotic-looking equipment was lined up along the wall, and five graduate students stood inside the curtain to observe the dean-worthy cases, of which I had become one.

I was in the dean's corner for almost an hour. Students called him away to consult about other patients, and I talked with the grad students while we waited for him to return.

"What made you want to go into optometry?" I asked them, and they told me about their childhood eye doctor or said one of their parents was an optometrist. The next time the dean left, I asked about local hiking trails. A student described hiking around a small lake, and two of the others asked questions. How long did it take to drive there? Where was the trailhead?

"I can show you," the first student said, and I felt triumphant: I was helping them connect.

The dean returned and had me sit in front of another robot for a while.

"I've never seen an eye like yours," he said. He meant in a thirty-year-old who had access to health care when she was a child.

At one point, the dean had me take a break to rest my eyes. He sat on a rolling stool, asked what I did, and said he loved teaching, too. I tried to include his grad students in our conversation, but they were only chatty when the dean left to examine other patients.

"Well, my dear," said the dean, when the robots and the two of us had done the best we could with my exam, "you have amblyopia—lazy eye. I don't know why it wasn't caught when you were young."

Lazy eye develops between the ages of four and nine, when a stronger eye takes over the work of vision and a weaker eye stops exerting itself. Without the need to focus, the weak eye might begin to wander in its socket. This is relatively easy to prevent: A child with amblyopia might wear a patch over their strong eye, forcing the lazy one to work harder. When I was young, kids wore beige medical patches. Now, children can wear a bright felt cover appliqued with a flower or dinosaur over one side of their glasses.

The dean said I was too old for the standard treatment, but if I ever lost vision in my right eye, even in adulthood, my left one could get slightly stronger. It would be forced to look at the world more clearly.

He wondered aloud again why my left eye wasn't flip-flopping around. And then he was silent for a moment. A murmur slid under the curtain from the row of exam chairs I had skimmed through earlier that morning.

"I suppose you use your left eye to communicate," the dean finally said. "Look at you this whole time, talking with my students. I've never seen them so relaxed." One student froze, one shuffled his feet, one lifted her hand to cover a smile, and I could see what each of them was feeling.

"There are vision training games for amblyopia," the dean said. He tapped his ophthalmoscope against his palm. "You didn't learn to focus your left eye, but you might have learned to move it in tandem with your right eye to communicate. I suppose you created your own game."

Tap, tap.

"Just a hunch," he said.

In the 1940s, Dr. Herman A. Witkin, a psychology professor at Brooklyn College, conducted research about vertical orientation: how people determine which direction is up. Witkin had just gotten married when the US Army asked him to move his research to the School of Aviation Medicine in Texas. They wanted him to figure out why some pilots flew out of the clouds with their feet toward the sky. (Herman's wife chose to stay in New York to continue her graduate work, and thank goodness for that: During her long career, Dr. Evelyn Witkin made discoveries about DNA that illuminated how cancer develops.)

Witkin and a colleague designed a moveable chair for their experiment. In a pitch-black room, a researcher would tilt the chair while a test subject tried to point a rod perfectly upright. Some people,

Witkin learned, used internal cues—sensations from their bodies—to decide which way was up. Other people relied on external cues. A darkened room did not offer the visual cues they needed when their chair was tilted, and they pointed their rods any which way.

Witkin called the people who relied on internal cues "field independent." They did not need the surrounding environment to tell them what to do. He called the people who could not align the rod vertically in a darkened room "field dependent." Without cues from the environment, they were lost. He called this being fused: Field-dependent people could not detach themselves from the outside world.

A field-dependent person might not feel her internal cues. She might accidentally spin her plane when surrounded by clouds. She might ignore a blurry eye.

I took my first eye test after I started kindergarten. Unless kids had vision problems, that's how they did it when I was young: You had to know the letters of the alphabet. My sister, Thora, one year older than me, waited with me in the hall outside the doctor's office. Our mother wasn't with us—I suppose she stayed with our two younger sisters in the car.

"When you get in there," Thora whispered, "look for the paper with letters on it. You have to memorize the letters on the bottom line."

"Why?" I asked her.

"It's a test. You have to do good on tests."

When my name was called, I took the nurse's hand and walked into the room. I looked at the eye chart and stared at the lowest line. It was easy to memorize the letters: Our parents had my sisters and me memorize Bible verses and hymns to sing together before meals.

During the exam, the doctor said, "Cover your right eye. What's the lowest line you can read?" I recited the bottom line on the chart, and he said I had perfect vision.

I didn't squint. I didn't have headaches. I learned to read in first grade like the other kids. No one except me noticed that, over the next few years, the vision in my left eye grew blurry. Not able to detach eye exams from my sister's advice to learn the bottom line of letters, I kept memorizing eye charts.

Thora had 20/20 vision in both eyes. For her, memorizing the letters was a harmless game. I don't know if my younger sister, Sigrid, received the same advice about eye charts, but one of her eyes was crossed, and she had corrective surgery when she was four. Without surgery, a crossed eye often becomes lazy; instead, Sigrid ended up with perfect vision.

My left eye was not crossed. It did not wander while I lavished people with questions and eye contact and did everything I could to make people connect with me.

I tried to be honest during a vision test only once when I was a child. In my high school physics class, where I was the only girl, the male teacher would call my name and say, "Come up here and be my lovely assistant." Besides being put on display, it meant I couldn't take notes. I believed, based on movies, that men would leave me alone if I wore glasses, but since I'd been faking vision tests for a decade and supposedly had perfect eyesight, I told my mother I was getting headaches from studying.

At the optometrist's, I tried my best when the doctor used the machine that looks like the head of a giant housefly, with four silver dials clustered around each lens. The optometrist clicked between two lenses that faced my left eye.

"One, or two? Two, or one?"

I tried to suss out the difference between the blurry letters. "Can I see them again?" I asked a few times.

The doctor sat twelve inches in front of me and breathed peppermint into my nose.

Click, click.

"I don't know," I apologized.

My indecision seemed to make him uncomfortable, so I started saying one or two randomly. Sometimes he would say, "Good." At the end of the ones and twos, he had me wear the chosen lens, cover my right eye, and read the chart with my left. If I glanced, I could decode a letter on the third line of the eye chart but never two letters in a row. My left eye wouldn't stay focused.

"Maybe my eye is tired," I suggested, and the optometrist said that happens sometimes. I got the glasses I wanted, but I stopped wearing them when I finished the high school physics class. They didn't work, not to retrain my vision or the physics teacher.

When educational psychologists began to study field dependence and independence in the 1950s, they discovered that different approaches to decision-making also affected student performance. Field-independent students liked to figure things out for themselves. They didn't need feedback from a teacher to know if they mastered a task.

By the time I became a public school teacher in the late 1980s, educators no longer used the phrase "field dependent" because it sounded needy. They called people like me "field sensitive," which sounds kindhearted and perceptive.

Field-sensitive students learn information the way it is taught by a teacher. When I taught in a public school not far from Seattle, my fourth graders studied Washington state history. If I asked, "What is the capital of Washington?" field-sensitive students would chime, "Olympia."

Field-independent students, however, might say, "W," as though I'd asked for the capital letter, or they might say, "DC," and pretend I'd asked about our nation's capital. A smarty-pants field-independent kid, knowing capital can mean highest, might call out, "Mount Rainier."

Field-independent students like to come up with their own answers.

Field-sensitive students want someone to tell them what they are supposed to do. They are, let's be honest, easier to teach.

Dr. Herman Witkin's research project outlasted the war by thirty years. He discovered that field-independent people, the kind who could fly upright without needing to visually orient themselves, also did not orient themselves socially. They did not make decisions based on what other people said or did.

Witkin said field-independent people have a strong sense of self. "Boundaries have been formed between an inner core, experienced as the self, and nonself," he and a co-author wrote in *Cognitive Styles: Essence and Origins*. Witkin characterized field-independent people as "showing initiative, responsibility-taking, self-reliance, and the ability to think for themselves."

In contrast, field-sensitive people are fused to other people and operate in the world from a place of nonself. They are socially oriented, Witkin wrote—in fact, they must develop social skills to gain "access to information . . . something they are not easily able to do on their own."

In Witkin's view, experiencing the world in this way is a deficiency. But his description reminds me of one of the Big Five personality traits: People who score high in agreeableness try to understand others' thoughts and feelings and make decisions based on those perceptions. Hardly a deficiency. Besides, people from other parts of the world value the non-self differently than Western scientists do. In Buddhism, enlightenment is *nirvana,* a state of non-self filled with interconnection. In Latin American culture, *familismo* means the individual is one with the family. Bantu people in central and southern Africa have a worldview that rejects individualism; Desmond Tutu translated this concept, *Ubuntu,* as "a person is a person through other persons."

When I was young, I used the pronoun *we* whenever an adult asked what I was doing. "We're building a rock town." My mother and her friends laughed and called it my royal *we*, but I meant my three sisters and me. Even if I was the only one playing outside under the tree, stacking pebbles into roads and buildings, I felt like a we.

Connecting with other people makes me feel whole. As a child, it made me sensitive to social norms, including gender conformity. I would have aced a multiple-choice test about how girls—white, middle class, Protestant ones—were supposed to look and act.

I was the second of four girls, like Laura Ingalls in the *Little House on the Prairie* books and Jo Marsh in *Little Women*. Laura, Jo, and Caddie Woodlawn, another literary hero, were free-spirited, strong-willed, and unrestrained. They did not act the way girls were supposed to act, which fascinated me.

Laura, Jo, and Caddie would have flown their planes upright. I wished I were independent like them, yet I knew I was more like Jo's sister, Beth—energized by making others happy. Born to be a nonself.

When I was four years old, almost five, I ran outside to find my mom after Sunday School. My older sister was playing behind the church, and my two-year-old sister was still in the nursery. Our mother, in maternity clothes again, stood with a dark-haired young woman who held a newborn. A toddler sat in the gravel at her feet with one arm wrapped around her leg.

"I'm exhausted," the dark-haired woman told my mother.

The toddler threw some gravel, so I sat down and turned the gravel into a game. After a while, I heard Mom offer me as a mother's helper to the dark-haired woman. She could pick me up after lunch two times a week that summer, and I would play with her toddler to give her a break.

"This one can entertain her little sister for hours at a time," my mother said, caressing my head while I sat in the gravel. "She can watch the baby, too, if you need to nap."

I smiled up at the woman. I probably told her she looked pretty.

My mother knew I enjoyed being helpful. On our drive home, she told me that was why she offered me to the exhausted woman, although now I wonder if she needed a break from my chatter.

When I went to the dark-haired woman's apartment, she sat on the couch, the baby napped in the bassinet, and I played on the rug with the toddler. The woman wanted to talk, and I liked being able to make her laugh.

Her husband was in the Navy. He was scheduled to leave for a six-month tour a few months after I started spending afternoons at their apartment, and the dark-haired woman told my mother she felt desperately lonely whenever her husband shipped out. She asked if she could have me for a whole week when he left, including overnight. By then I was five, and my youngest sister had been born. I stood next to Mom while she nursed the baby. I ran to get her a glass of water. I handed her the safety pin when she was done so she could mark the next-feeding side of her bra. My mother didn't tell me to do those things. To me, it felt like play.

The dark-haired woman put a cot for me between her children's cribs and let me have Apple Jacks for breakfast. My job was to help her feel happy. At the end of the week, Mom picked me up. My baby sister was crying in a basket on the floor—this was before car seats. I pulled her out of the basket and sang to her while our mother drove us home.

Before I studied education and learned about field sensitivity and field independence, I assumed everyone was connection-seeking like me. But Witkin and other Western scientists who studied cognition seemed to think field independence was the norm.

In fact, Herman Witkin seemed baffled by the social skills of field-sensitive people. In a 1977 paper in *The Review of Educational Research,* Witkin and his co-authors mused that field-sensitive people seem "interested in what others say and do." They have "what in effect amounts to a sensitive radar system, selectively attuned to social components in the environment." They "literally look more at the faces of others." They are "drawn to people, in the sense of liking to be with them."

One of Witkin's colleagues, Philip Oltman, pointed out that field-sensitive people do well at cocktail parties. Although, he implied, why would anyone want to attend a cocktail party? In *Field Dependence in Psychological Theory, Research, and Application,* Oltman described feeling "backed into a corner by otherwise charming persons who had a preferred interpersonal space just a little too close for comfort."

I do enjoy a tangle of interpersonal space. If I were to show up at a party and someone else was wearing the same outfit as me, I would think, *oh, good.*

In my early parenting years, I learned the saying, "We need to teach our children to conform just enough to not incur the wrath of society." I wanted that for my kid: only the most necessary conformity.

And my kid, Indigo, seemed to understand the assignment. The parenting magazines said if I swept the kitchen, I should give my child a small broom because children love to copy their parents. I did not find that to be true.

One Saturday morning, my husband, Jason, took four-year-old Indigo to Mini Soccer so I could go to brunch with friends. Afterward, Jason asked, "Does our kid ever do what the other kids do?"

My toddler decorated Tonka trucks with ribbons and made bracelets out of earthworms. In preschool, the boys thought my child was a boy and the girls thought my child was a girl.

When the preschool teacher said, "Indigo marches to a different drummer," I wanted to pump my fist in the air.

In middle school, Indigo came out as transgender; later, they came out as nonbinary and switched to they/them pronouns. This was before trans kids were in the news, before Caitlyn Jenner came out. When Indigo told Jason and me, I didn't feel surprised. In fact, a month before our child told us, "Mom, Dad, I'm transgender," I had asked them if they were. Middle schoolers don't want their mothers to see inside them, though, and Indigo snapped at me. Reading social cues too loudly can get one into trouble.

When Indigo was ready to come out publicly, I unleashed my social skills. Since people are visual and love a good story, I wrote a booklet filled with pictures of my baby growing up. I called the parents of Indigo's friends and scheduled a staff meeting at the preschool I had opened after Indigo started school. I was not hesitant. I was bold, like Laura, Jo, and Caddie.

I smiled and hugged the folks who were the cloud around my child because I needed them to feel connected. Out for drinks one night with friends, I told the group about Indigo, clinked the glass of a conservative acquaintance, and said, "Cheers!"

"Cheers," she echoed, without thinking, as I knew she would, which got everyone around the table clinking and cheering for my baby. I did not care if I was being manipulative; I only cared about Indigo.

Recently, when I thought about the pilots who could not keep their airplanes right side up in the clouds, I wondered if today's planes offer warning beeps or flashing lights if a pilot starts to spin. My father-in-law, Bill, owned a Cessna when my husband was young, so I emailed him.

"How do airplanes let the pilot know the plane is upside down when there's no visibility?"

"Your body will certainly tell you," Bill wrote back. "Straining against your seatbelt. Blood rushing to your head."

Clearly, my father-in-law is field independent.

A decade after Herman Witkin died, Thomas Carretta, a staff psychologist at the Air Force Research Laboratory, recreated the Embedded Figures Test—a successor to Witkin's tilted-chair experiment. Carretta evaluated two thousand pilot candidates and concluded that neither field sensitivity nor field independence determined a pilot's performance value. The Air Force had different kinds of planes, he wrote in Technical Paper 87-36, and needed different kinds of pilots.

Field sensitivity is better for multi-person crews because people like me—so tuned in to others—work well with a team. The Air Force would never put that on a recruiting poster, though: "Multi-person crews—the place where a non-self will thrive."

Field independence is better for pilots who fly fast jets. Laura, Jo, Caddie—they would have flown those. They would notice if blood rushed to their heads or if they had a blurry eye.

I wonder what it would feel like to disregard a cloud or to ignore the feelings of the person sitting next to you. Freeing, I suppose. But if I could trade my field sensitivity for perfect vision, would it make me less able to see other people? Less fascinated by our differences? Would I have been less able to see my child?

Was I a self or a non-self when I became a mama bear for Indigo? Maybe I was neither. Or both. Maybe by wanting to help my child, I rose above the binary.

FOUR WORDS

Our mother always told the truth, except that morning in the car. Her words that day were quiet and good, yet they were a lie. Also, they taught me I could choose what I believe.

Our mother always told the truth is an exaggeration. Virtually everyone lies. In a study that asked people to keep a daily journal, even the most truthful respondents admitted to lying up to two times a day.

From the driver's seat, our father said, "Can it," but Sigrid, who was ten years old, said one more bratty thing. (Let me ease your mind: My sister did not get hit that day.)

"Sigrid," our mother warned, without turning around in the passenger seat.

Right then, the car shuddered onto the gravel at

the side of the freeway. We strained against our lap belts while our father braked, and I thought we had a flat tire until I realized he was screaming at Sigrid.

Our father was over six feet tall, weighed more than two hundred pounds, and I didn't want his anger directed at me, so the most I would let myself do was reach into my sister's lap to hold her hand. That small act, though not enough, meant something, too.

I didn't want his anger directed at me. Psychologist Lawrence Kohlberg developed a theory with three levels of moral development. The first level, Preconventional, is egocentric: Children and some adults behave based on a fear of punishment or desire for reward.

The car halted with a whomp. A giant arm swung back toward Sigrid, who pressed into me where I sat, hard to reach, behind the driver's seat. Eight-year-old Greta leaned against the opposite window while our father's hand flailed through the air.

"Get up here," he yelled.

A swat on Sigrid's bottom would have seemed fair, but the way his screaming bulged the car windows, I knew she would get a beating, not a smack. I also knew our mother would not intervene. Our mother believed in the will of God, whose will is to command as ours is to obey.

Regarding the ethics of lying, *the will of God* is debatable. The Bible says, "All liars shall have their place in the lake which burns with fire and brimstone" (Revelations 21:8). Yet it also says, "God shall send them strong delusion, that they should believe a lie" (2 Thessalonians 2:11).

Sometimes Mom read to us from Corrie ten Boom's *The Hiding Place,* a memoir from World War II. In one scene, Corrie's niece tells the truth when German soldiers raid the family's home.

"Where are your men?" the soldiers demand.

"They're under the table," the little girl says. She laughs when a soldier flips up the tablecloth and no one is there. (Two people hid under a trap door under the rug under the table. During the Holocaust, Corrie ten Boom's family smuggled hundreds of Jews to safety.)

After the soldiers leave, the ten Boom family argues about whether the little girl should have lied instead of being honest.

"God honors truth-telling with perfect protection," Corrie's sister says.

My mother believed those words. She believed in obedience for all of us. It was always wrong to lie.

It was always wrong to lie. Potential repercussions for the liar include: 1) feeling bad about oneself, 2) not being considered trustworthy, 3) having to keep one's story straight, 4) a downward spiral into pathological lying, 5) becoming separated from reality by believing one's own lies, and 6) hellfire and damnation.

Our father turned off the engine and started counting. Sigrid had ten seconds to climb into the front seat, where at least the hitting would be restrained by the roof of the car and by our mother's body in the passenger seat while she stared straight ahead.

"Five," our father continued.

Our mother's voice was quiet as a closed box, yet my sisters and I could hear her words while we burrowed into the back seat.

"You can't hit her."

"Six."

"She started her period." Four words. Seven syllables.

The counting stopped, and we waited. He could go off again. Sigrid's body was rigid against me, and I didn't dare swing my eyes to look at Greta.

Our mother's voice did not waver, though it was barely audible. "You could damage her internal organs."

You could damage her internal organs is a lie of embellishment. When a detail that is or could be true is linked to a false statement, it can create the illusion of truth.

Cars from the freeway shook my window while we waited on the gravel shoulder. After a while, our father deflated. He turned the key in the ignition, and we drove onto the freeway. I kept holding Sigrid's hand.

By the time we reached our friends' house, we were back to normal, the way we looked in Christmas card photos: a bunch of yellow-haired girls and their parents, neatly arranged in their church clothes. Or maybe the explosions were our normal. Either way, everything had changed.

Sigrid had not started her period. Our mother had told a lie.

Everything had changed is hyperbole. Some statements are so grandiose they are not meant to be understood as true.

When we returned from visiting our friends, I told my older sister, Thora, about that morning in the car. She was fourteen and allowed to stay home on her own. I whispered the story in her bedroom, and Thora stared at me, then laughed.

"That means he can't hit us anymore," she said.

That means he can't hit us anymore is a conclusion based on a false premise, also known as an unsound argument. An unsound argument is not necessarily untrue.

"I haven't started my period," I told her.

"Me neither, but he doesn't know that."

Later that summer, my period did start. I was at gymnastics practice and, after wondering for several minutes if I were dying, decided it must be menstrual blood even though it was dark brown. I imagined it turned from red to brown because, that first time on its journey, it took a long time to find its way out.

I made a pad out of toilet paper, rolled more paper around the leg openings in my underwear to hold the pad in place, and hoped the contraption wouldn't show through my leotard. I didn't think about calling my mother. I didn't tell her when I got home.

My sisters and I knew about periods and penises and vaginas. Our mom didn't believe in telling children lies about the stork bringing babies or finding them under a cabbage.

The stork bringing babies is an example of lies-to-children. Parents, priests, parliaments, and the police tell lies of this kind, insisting they must protect those who do not have the mental or emotional strength to handle the truth. Lying to children or child-like people is for their own good, the powerful tell themselves. In contrast, the lies told by child-like people might be a survival mechanism.

Years earlier, around the time I started school, our mother had bought a giant box of Kotex, the kind that clipped to an elastic belt around the waist. She put it under our bathroom sink and said she didn't want us to worry about supplies, but as we grew closer to period-age, she stopped talking about puberty. There were many things our mother did not talk about.

The *many things our mother did not talk about* were lies of omission. By not naming what happened inside our family, my parents allowed my sisters and me to believe every family was like ours.

Over the next few months, I used up most of the pads in the box.

One morning, Thora visited my bedroom.

"Did you get your period?" she asked. She had just gotten hers and discovered the mostly empty box under the sink. "Did you tell Mom?"

"No. Did you?"

"No, but we're gonna need more pads," Thora said. Although she had a newspaper route and I babysat, we didn't want to spend our money on supplies.

We planned how to tell our mother and practiced the sentence, each of us saying every other word. My words were: Mom, have, our. Thora's words were: we, started, periods.

At the time, I didn't think this way of announcing our bodies were changing was strange, nor the way our mother had no questions. It fit the silences in our family.

I have read about a family in Northern California that hosted a celebration in the forest the night after their child's first cycle appeared.

"Now you are a giver of life," the eldest family member told the menstruating child, and everyone danced together under the moonlight.

Our mother said she would buy us another box of Kotex, and Thora and I asked for the kind with adhesive. Later, we asked for tampons, although that negotiation took a few years. Some people at our family's church said tampons take a girl's virginity, and while our mother knew that wasn't accurate, still, she hesitated. She was raised to not question authority.

Tampons take a girl's virginity is a crazy-ass lie.

Every morning, my mother sat in her chair in the living room. Her chair matched our father's, except it was smaller. She opened her Bible and daily devotional, read the verses and homily for the day, bowed her head for one minute, closed both books, and that was that.

Sometimes I watched her from the hallway. It looked like another chore, another rule to follow. Read the Bible. Do not take the name of the Lord in vain. Do not wear your church dress outside to play. Never lie: There is never a good reason, not even if you are hiding Jews.

There is never a good reason, not even if you are hiding Jews is an example of traditional ethics. Rules before relationships. Laws before love. Justice is blind.

Until that morning in the car when Dad braked on the side of the freeway, our mother had always behaved as if right and wrong were absolute. It did not matter if a rule made sense, or if there were mitigating circumstances, or if a child was crying.

Our father was rarely home, so our mother did most of the hitting, and even her hitting had rules. She used the flat side of the hairbrush, never the bristle side. She never hit us when we were naked. She never slapped our faces because that would be disrespectful.

"If God didn't want you to have spankings, why did he give you a bottom?" she would say, but a few swats would do, quick and efficient. Most of the time, when she touched us, it was a cuddle, a kiss, and a hug.

If God didn't want you to have spankings, why did he give you a bottom? is an example of either bullshitting or a non sequitur.

I did not feel afraid of my mother. When I was three, she bit my shoulder because I wouldn't stop biting Thora. It hurt, but I was not scared. I remember feeling offended: I knew at age three that mothers should not bite their children.

I followed the rules when my parents were watching—no, I made it look like I followed the rules. I told lies long before my mother told hers.

I lied to get out of trouble, to make a story more exciting, if I didn't know the truth but wanted people to think I did, to cover for my sisters, just because I could.

One kindergarten recess, I crawled under the yellow caution tape that blocked the ladder to our outdoor play loft and climbed to the top, where the school custodian had left an open can of paint. When the boy who said mean things to girls started playing near the loft, I tipped the paint over so it sploshed onto his pale crew cut. It was easy to sneak down the ladder and join the crowd of children.

When the teacher arrived, I told her, wide-eyed, "Someone poured paint on Roger."

Someone poured paint on Roger is a partial truth. Benjamin Franklin said, "Half a truth is a great lie."

Thora could not lie very well. Friedrich Nietzsche suggested some people are too scatter-brained to lie and others, too cowardly. For the record, Nietzsche was opposed to lying.

My sister is both brave and brilliant, but she is a strong introvert. Unlike me, she lacked the experience with social engagement that effective liars subconsciously use to build their skills.

Social engagement that effective liars subconsciously use to build their skills: Mine included using my upturned face, smile, eye contact, and not too much detail. Early on, I learned if people liked me, they would trust me, and I was raised to be likeable. My ability to lie, of course, was further propped up by privilege: Little white girls are assumed to be innocent.

One time, when we were eight and nine years old, Thora said, "Goddamn it," while we played in the front yard. When we came inside, my sister called into the kitchen to our mother, "Did you hear what I said?"

I stopped at the front doorway. What was she doing?

"No, I didn't hear. What did you say?" our mother asked.

Thora could have said she called our mother the prettiest mom. She could have said we were reciting Bible verses. If she had to confess to a swear word, she could have claimed only the "damn." Swearing with God's name was a terrible sin, for which Thora got her mouth washed out with soap, because she couldn't lie.

Thora got her mouth washed out with soap. Washing a child's mouth with soap was intended to both deter lying and symbolically purify the child's speech. Traditional Christian ethics considered the child's fear and humiliation, as well as the terrible taste, a small price if it prevented future immorality. Some Christians refer to the "Millstone" verse: "If anyone causes one of these little ones . . .

to stumble, it would be better for them to have a large millstone hung around their neck and to be drowned in the depths of the sea" (Matthew 18:6).

Two years later, when I was ten, I told my mother, "I'm never going to hit my children."

I'm never going to hit my children. Is a promise to oneself a lie since it has not yet and may never come true?

Mom kept her hands moving in the sink but looked at me when she said, "I remember thinking that when I was your age. Every child feels that way."

She scrubbed hard at the pot, not needing to look at it to know where to use the steel wool. "When you grow up, you'll understand. You'll want to raise your children to be good."

I did not argue with her, but I decided that I would be the first human being ever who did not hit her children. I didn't know if it was possible.

A few years later, that morning in the car, my mother's four-word lie opened many possibilities.

My mother's four-word lie opened many possibilities. Possible benefits to the liar included: 1) gaining a sense of agency, 2) showing her children their safety mattered more to her than telling the truth, 3) revealing to herself she was capable of independent thought, and 4) teaching her children they had the right to choose the rules they would follow, the lives they would lead.

When Sigrid was four, she had surgery and got to spend a week alone with our mother. When she was six, the principal bumped her up a grade in school. Our mother held Sigrid's hand, and they walked out to the recess yard where Thora, Greta, and I waited on the swings.

"I'm proud to announce your sister will skip second grade," our mother said.

I was jealous, not so much because Sigrid got a toy for having surgery or because she skipped a grade but because I craved our mother's attention. I wanted to spend a week with her, even if it were in the hospital.

Thora decided she no longer liked our second-youngest sister, and soon I followed. I ignored Sigrid when she called my name. I threw rolled-up socks at her. I pretended it hurt my skin if she brushed against me. When we got in the car that morning and Sigrid climbed over Greta to get to the middle, I drew a line with my finger across the seat as a barrier she could not cross.

I pretended it hurt my skin if she brushed against me is gaslighting, a form of lying that makes the victim doubt reality. It's what sociopaths and cult leaders do. It is a lie of cruelty. My shuddering told my sister that her body, her *self*, was unlovable. I pretended it so hard that I lied to myself, until that morning in the car.

When I grabbed Sigrid's hand that day, I noticed I felt different before we finished braking. I remember the lightness of realizing I loved my sister. How strange it is that fear can lead to love.

While Sigrid was fused to my side, she gripped my hand and panted, and as much as my own body tightened with fear, I knew it did not match my sister's terror. At thirteen, I understood I could keep a giant hand from flailing at me by acting pleasant.

Acting pleasant is a euphemism for being submissive. A euphemism is rarely regarded as a lie.

My fear arose from knowing I was weak—too small to stop our father's hands and too cowardly to cover Sigrid's body with my own.

After that car ride, though, our father's hands could no longer hit us or he would damage our internal organs. Our mother had to follow the same rule since a wife must follow her husband.

About a year after I told Thora what happened in the car, she shut my bedroom door and sat on my bed after a fight with our mother.

"Did you hear Mom? She lectured me for an hour. I wish she would just smack me," my older sister said.

During my teen years, I thought about the lie that protected my younger sister. It meant our mother loved us more than the rules she believed in. It meant that sometimes it is better to lie.

Sometimes it is better to lie. Ethicist Carol Gilligan proposed an alternative to traditional ethics, one concerned more with compassion than unwavering rules. Gilligan called it the ethics of care. If the only way for a mother to protect her child is to lie, the Ethics of Care says it is better to lie.

Because my mother did not talk with my sisters and me about what happened in our family when we were at home, I thought every man acted like my father when the front door was closed.

Our mother did not talk about what happened at home. Lies of omission create secrets. Does that mean all secrets are lies?

A few years after that morning in the car, I rode my bike to my friend Jackie's house. She wasn't home yet from basketball practice.

"Let's have some lemonade," her mother said, and I helped her carry a tray with glasses out to the patio.

The Walkers went to the same church as my family, and Mrs. Walker asked how youth group was going and what her daughter and I planned to do that afternoon. I chattered, and we were quiet for a while. Then she began talking about her childhood in Alaska.

"The men were very rough," she said. Her brothers, her father, the men all around her were rough.

"I decided when I was about your age that I wouldn't get married unless I found a gentle man. I didn't know if there were any." She said when she met Mr. Walker, she tested his kindness for several years before she agreed to marry him.

I knew Jackie's dad. He taught fourth grade. I could almost imagine him being gentle when no one outside his family was watching.

Mrs. Walker did not say she was aware of what happened behind our closed family door, although

I realize now she must have known. If she had asked if my father was rough, I would have lied. I was trained to lie about that. Instead, Mrs. Walker opened a new door for me and let me peek through.

I was trained to lie about that. I would not have lied directly. I would have obfuscated, as my mother did when her friend helped pull thorns out of my baby sister's legs, and Mom said, "He was so clumsy, dropping Greta in the cactus like that," instead of, "What kind of father shields himself with his child when he falls?" One wonders about the ethics of training children to lie while insisting that lying is a sin.

Later, at a Christian youth retreat Jackie and I attended, light from the overhead projector filled the screen with a black-and-white illustration. The hand of God held a hammer. The hammer was the father, who pounded a chisel. The chisel was the mother, who chipped at a diamond. The diamond was the child.

It is only now, decades after seeing that black-and-white illustration, that I realize the chisel had once been a diamond. So had the hammer.

Why did my mother choose that morning in the car to tell a lie, when her three youngest daughters were in the back seat, when tires scrubbed against the gravel, when our friends waited an hour away?

Why, on that morning, did she aim the chisel away from her child?

I wonder if someone opened a door for my mother and told her it was possible. Or maybe, after years of believing she must follow the rules, she understood they were not working.

After years of believing she must follow the rules is an example of Kohlberg's second level, Conventional, when moral reasoning is concerned with social norms and law and order.

One night, when I was in high school and helping my mother with dinner, she told me that, years before, she had asked a church pastor for advice about our father. "I told the pastor everything," she said. My mother always moved quickly in the kitchen—washing, peeling, pouring, sponging—but I remember she stood still for a moment and looked down at her hands, which rested on the counter. "He said I must submit as commanded by the Apostle Paul."

Maybe she created her own opening when she told the lie. Maybe when she stopped hitting her children as she'd been raised to do, it made the passage big enough for her to call out to her pastor. Why did my mother believe she needed one man's permission to leave another?

Maybe she created her own opening. If lies can be threads in "a tangled web we weave, / When first we practice to deceive," might they also form a rope ladder one can climb toward freedom?

During college, at home on a break, I read a story by Harry Belafonte in my mother's *Guideposts* magazine. The Belafontes had decided they would never hit their children, and now they had grandchildren—two generations who would never be hit.

I knew it could be done, I thought. But I hadn't known, I had only hoped. I needed Harry Belafonte to show me it was possible.

In college, although I'd had enough of right and wrong, the only humanities class that fit my schedule was Ethics 101. The professor said people weigh values differently and had us debate which was worth more: freedom or safety? Fostering community or self-actualization? Growing vegetables or creating art?

He quoted from Joseph Fletcher's *Situation Ethics*. Fletcher said people should respect the rules they were raised to follow but "set them aside in the situation if love seems better served by doing so." And I thought, *oh, that is what I believe.* That morning when we swerved to the side of the freeway, my mother's lie told me I did not have to unthinkingly follow the rules.

I did not have to unthinkingly follow the rules. Kohlberg's final level, Post-Conventional, prioritizes social justice: Rules should adapt to the different needs of individuals.

One evening in college, my roommate had a friend over, and I ate dinner with the two of them.

The friend said she was thinking about buying a moped but was scared of the campus police.

"They seem to go after mopeds," she said.

"Yeah," I said, "I got a ticket yesterday for riding on the back of one."

My roommate, Kris, knew the story: Months earlier, I had gotten a warning, not a ticket. She waited until her friend left before asking me, "Why did you lie about it?"

"You lie about stuff that doesn't even matter," Kris said, which was true. Lying felt easy. Familiar.

Why did you lie about it? At the time, I did not know, but now I understand I told the lie to connect. My lie was harmless, a white lie, changing a few details to let Kris's friend know I understood her fear. White lies are intended to bring people closer. "I love your new haircut," we say.

I could have denied Kris's accusation. I could have said I misspoke or you heard me wrong or no, what I meant was—

Lying was a shelter when I was a child, and my mother's lie gave me permission to continue. My lies hid beneath the pleasantness I wore like a church dress, but I didn't want to pretend anymore. It was my last year of college, and I wanted to put away childish things.

"Yeah," I told Kris, "I lie a lot."

"Don't do it to me," she said, and I practiced telling the truth until it began to feel ordinary, like breathing in.

I practiced telling the truth. Right out of college, while living in San Francisco, I paid for hot tea so I could sit at grimy bistro tables and write in my spiral notebook. I tried to write honestly, although truthful writing in my twenties meant revealing other people's falsehoods, not my own.

I still try to tell the truth, but I love to tell stories. If it makes the story better to say it happened on a Tuesday instead of on a Wednesday, I will not be a purist. I will tell the better story.

Here is a true story about lying. A shorebird called the killdeer will try to lure a predator away from the eggs in its nest by pretending to have a broken wing. If the drama of the broken wing does not distract the predator, the killdeer will fluff up its feathers and raise its tail to make itself look bigger.

Pretending to have a broken wing is a lie of bluffing. There's bluffing, and then there is double bluffing, like when I tell people I am terrible at poker because I'm too expressive, then bluff my way to a winning hand, which has happened only once because, the truth is, I am terrible at poker.

My mother's childhood in a religious boarding school was filled with unbreakable rules. Among the litany, she was taught that a wife must submit to her husband, to put him first in all things or be cast into hell. My mother risked hell for her child.

My mother risked hell for her child. Besides believing she must obey her husband, my mother believed the "Millstone" verse: She must keep her children on heaven's path. Inspired by the same verse, in 2023, an Oklahoma senator sponsored the Millstone Act to criminalize gender-based health care for transgender youth. South Carolina and Texas soon followed with their own Millstone legislation. In a group chat about one of the bills, a supporter said, "I'd rather my kid be dead than transgender. At least [my child] won't go to hell."

After my sisters and I grew up and left home, our parents joined a new church. Once more our mother told a pastor about our father, but this time, the pastor said divorce is allowed in certain circumstances. Within a year, our mother left our father.

What if Mom had believed what I knew as a child, that our father had no right to beat his daughters? What if the truth had grown so strong within her that she told him, "Stop, or I will leave you"?

My mother's childhood makes mine feel like playing dodgeball at recess. Sometimes I got hit, but mostly it was laughing and whooping with my playmates and sisters.

On our sister Zoom a few weeks ago, with all of us now in our fifties and living in four different places, we talked about the time our mother told a lie. Even Thora remembered, and she wasn't in the car.

"It was big," said Greta. "It was big," we echoed.

"Did Mom ever talk to you about that day?" I asked. I meant my question for Sigrid, but all three of my sisters shook their heads, no, on the screen.

I looked at Sigrid's box and said, "I remember holding your hand."

"Yeah," she said.

I wanted her to say it made her feel safe. I will always be thirteen, wishing to be brave enough to save my sister.

Our mother is almost ninety now. She has the sweet kind of Alzheimer's, the kind that makes my sisters and me say, "We're so lucky." Dementia seems to have freed her from the litany of her childhood, and she is now the happiest I've known her to be.

Dementia seems to have freed her. Jesus said, "The truth shall set you free," yet Alzheimer's seems to have done that for my mother, and my mother's lie did that for me.

When I visit my mother in memory care, I can't stop myself from petting her hair and rubbing her shoulders. Sometimes she remembers she has four daughters, although usually she laughs as though I'm giving her a present.

"I am the mother?" she said the other day. "That's such a surprise to me."

My sisters and I never asked our mom about the time she told a lie, and now it is too late. Except that now, because of her Alzheimer's, we hold our weekly sister Zooms. We ask each other what we remember from our childhood. We say important things out loud the way our mother did not, except for the time when she stared straight ahead before turning to face our father.

LET US SIT ON THE LAWN

A few weeks after Indigo came out to us as transgender, a little more than a decade ago, our family attended a Gender Diversity meeting at Seattle Children's Hospital. Indigo, who was fourteen, joined the teens in the big room, and Jason and I opened the door to the parent room, where a box of Kleenex was circling.

Parents whose children come out as transgender often feel overwhelmed with grief. They might say something unkind, raise their voices, and refuse to leap beyond the way they've always understood gender. Weeks or years later, many will come around and use the right name and pronouns, and some will even delight in the expansion of their world.

Jason and I were different. I was scared about the world outside our home, but when Indigo said, "Mom, Dad, I'm transgender," I wanted to shout hallelujah.

"It's like finding the pieces of a puzzle," Jason said.

During introductions at the parent group, I spoke for the two of us, as I do, and afterward the group's founder, Aidan Key, raised his hand to share that it was the first time he'd heard parents say they celebrated. Around the same time, friends who were watching our life from the bleachers—whose children were not trans—told us we were exemplary parents, and I enjoyed believing them.

A few years ago, I trained as a facilitator for Aidan's support group, which is now national, online, and called TransFamilies. I worried I wouldn't feel compassion for the mothers and fathers in their little Zoom boxes, but at my first observation session, my smugness fell away. Parents did cry, misgender their children, and talk about losing the child they knew—but their desperate love for their babies was palpable.

My love for my child was not bigger than theirs.

I was raised with a different language.

For a homework assignment when I was twelve, I asked my mother to share a memory from when she was my age.

"*Siéntate,*" she said, and I pulled out my chair at the kitchen table.

Mom squeezed two glasses of orange juice before joining me. She would have picked the oranges that morning in our California backyard.

"I remember lying in my bed every night," she said, handing me a glass. She meant her bed in the dorm at the boarding school she attended in Quito. My mother grew up in Ecuador, where her Scandinavian parents ran a school for Indigenous boys.

"I would pray to God to make me a boy."

I remember feeling sorry for my mom that God had not made her a boy, yet I did not feel surprised. My mother scrubbed her lipstick off as soon as she shut the car door after church. She walked with her elbows triangled out, not held close to her sides the way other women walked. As a child, I'd assumed this was because she didn't grow up in America and did not know the rules.

I knew my mom did things differently because she was an immigrant. She fed us cut-up jicama for snacks and let us walk barefoot to the store. To tell us she was joking, she said, "I'm screwing you," instead of "screwing with you." My mother's oddities allowed my three siblings and me to be ourselves when we were not at church or school. We were supposed to be loud and get dirty; she never told us to be careful. Our mother grew up in the jungle.

She was born in Riobamba, Ecuador, near the Chimborazo volcano. If you were to climb to the top of Chimborazo, you would stand on the land that is farthest from the center of the Earth. In my mother's stories, she lived in an enchanted forest. She was free to play near the river and explore "two trees" off the path.

"If I went more than two trees, I would be lost forever."

At seven, she was sent to a boarding school run by missionaries, where she became fluent in Spanish and English. The children were divided into girls' and boys' dormitories, and girls and boys had different rules for their behavior. My mother was taught to conform, although the coating of conformity did not permeate her marrow.

A few years ago, I watched a documentary about the brand of religious schools my mother had attended. No wonder she kept her prayers to herself.

Some of the children who lived in the dorms had a harder time pretending to conform. "They were difficult," my mother said. "The houseparents didn't like them." Now, having raised a child and taught for more than thirty years, I know there is more to that story, but when I was young, I did not question my mother's words.

Several years ago, I read an article by a trans woman who described the thrill of seeing pink and sparkly things when she was a child, and I thought, *oh, I remember.* I was assigned female at birth, and I loved being a girl. My insides felt giddy if I saw a picture of a ballerina. When I was six years old and my family was on the It's a Small World ride at Disneyland, I sat on my knees in the boat and leaned over the edge, gazing at the girl dolls. I wanted to be one of them.

One of my sisters was gender conforming like me. Two were not.

We used to say there were two brothers and two sisters in our family, although we said it only to each other.

In a town where we lived for a year, one sister told the neighborhood kids her name was Steve. For her birthday, our mother took her to Sears to buy Toughskins.

"She let me try them on in the boys' department," Steve told me.

On our last day in that town, while the moving truck was being packed, we rode our bikes nearby with the neighbor kids until our father yelled out the four girl names he had given us.

"Get your bikes in the truck."

Three of us biked back, but Steve kept playing. Our dad called out her girl name again. Finally, Steve wheeled her bike around and rode toward the moving van while the neighborhood boys called out, "You're a girl? You're a girl!" I didn't know how to do more than stare at them while Steve rode up into the truck.

Steve says she doesn't remember much about her childhood.

In a different town, my mom said she would make curtains and quilts for the room another sibling and I shared. I will call that sibling Alex. I wanted a feminine fabric but was sure my mother would choose something neutral since Alex hated girly stuff. Mom sewed while we were at school, and one afternoon, I walked into our room with no hint from my mother about what I would see. She had hung our new curtains and made up our beds. My quilt and curtains were pink, covered with purple ballerinas. Alex's fabric was stars and stripes, red, white, and blue. Our curtains met in the middle of the window.

I knew those curtains were unconventional. I knew the world outside our home was easier for me than for Steve or Alex or my mother. Sometimes I would try to teach my family to conform. This is how to be a girl. But like our rolled-up sock fights and jicama and the fact that we could recite the books of the Bible forward and backward by the time we were six, their diversity was the air I breathed in.

Young children think their families are the norm; as they move toward adolescence, they begin to uncover the distinctions.

Once, when I was a fifth-grade teacher, the sunny afternoon in our classroom south of Seattle lured me into letting an eleven-year-old tell a long story during math time about how his mother had snuck a bunny into their apartment. He was a sweetheart, the youngest of seven, the only one born in America.

"My mom is so weird," he said.

"Every family is weird," I told the boy. I said this at least once a school year and watched each crop of fifth graders relax into those words.

When I was in ninth grade, we attended a drab Presbyterian church where the congregants sat motionless while they sang. In our Sunday School classroom, unless an adult made us mix, the girls hung out on one side and the boys on the other. A kid named Brenda would sit against the wall between the two groups, head on her arms, which were folded on her knees, which spread wide like a boy. I tried to get her to join our group, but even with all my girly charm, I could not.

Two years later, my mother let me go to a different church. I told her it was for the music, though really it was because I wanted a larger selection of boys. My mom and Brenda's mother, Peggy, were friends, and Mom kept me apprised of my classmate from Sunday School. Brenda ran away from home. She was hospitalized and endured rounds of conversion therapy. She tried to kill herself.

"Peggy called," Mom said one winter afternoon when I was in high school. "I need to tell you."

She made us tea, letting me choose the kind. She was quiet until we sat at the table.

"Peggy says Brenda is turning into a boy." The family would move to San Francisco where their child could have surgery. "They're not telling anyone. They're saying Jim got a new job."

No one would know what had been before.

"Peggy said she has to choose between the church and her child, and she's choosing her child." My mother's voice sounded warm, like my peppermint tea.

I pictured how Brenda used to slouch, miserable behind the hair that was not allowed to be cut. Although the news my mother told me felt extreme, it also felt correct. Wouldn't a girl have wanted to join our side of the room in Sunday School?

I don't know if I had forgotten about my mom praying to be a boy when she told me about Brenda, or why I did not connect Brenda's diversity to my family. Maybe it was because it was the 1970s, and I had only heard the phrase "sex change" whispered, the same way older women at church would say "cancer." Gender diversity—though no one called it that back then—was said to be incredibly rare. (It is not. In 2024, the CDC published a national survey in which more than 3 percent of US high schoolers identified themselves as transgender.)

When my child, Indigo, was young, they did not conform to gender norms. Indigo wore a tutu with overalls to preschool and loved both dinosaurs and Polly Pockets. After Indigo transitioned, a girlfriend gave me a copy of an email I had sent when our children were young: "There are boys and there are girls and there is my kid."

All of that felt normal to me.

Most of the time, I made room for my child's gender creativity, but sometimes I would style their hair to look, if not like their gender assigned at birth, at least more unisex. And for a family photo when Indigo was eight, I tricked my child into dressing like their assigned gender.

The night before our appointment, I dropped the outfit I wanted Indigo to wear in the corner of their room as though my child had already worn it. When we were rushing to leave for the studio the next morning, I said to my child, "You need to wear clean clothes. Why don't you throw those on?" And this is the evil part: I made sure Indigo did not see a mirror before we took the photo. I did not know my child was transgender. I did not know happy children could be trans. But I knew my child did not want to look the way I tricked them to be.

Indigo screamed at me when they saw the photo. Jason and I did not allow our child to yell at us: You can be gender creative but not disrespectful. I didn't call my child on the screaming that day, however, because I knew—I had known all along—that forcing my child to conform was wrong.

"I'll never make you wear clothes like that again," I told my baby.

I did not know Indigo was trans or genderqueer or nonbinary. I didn't have the language, so I would say, "Not a boy, not a girl." Years later, though, when Indigo said the words, "Mom, Dad, I'm transgender," I was ready. It never felt like a loss to me. It felt like the final click that opens a safe.

"Would you still love me if I realized I were a man?" I asked Jason a few weeks after our child transitioned.

I thought his response would take a while. When one is married to an introvert, one learns to wait for hours, or days, or forever. But he said yes immediately.

"Would you still love me if I were a woman?" he asked.

"That'd be great," I said, which may not have been the optimal answer, but he is used to me.

I told each of my family members about Indigo coming out as trans in a one-on-one conversation. My mother, my sister formerly known as Steve, and my sibling whom I am calling Alex each said something like, "I wish I could have done that."

I said they still could, but I wasn't really thinking of them. I was imagining how it would make things easier for my child. We could have a Cedar family trans team.

"I don't need to change," said my mom. "When you get older, the men act more like women and the women act more like men."

Formerly Steve said, "I figure I'm agender."

Alex said, "It would have made my life so much better."

Alex and I sat on the lawn in a park in Seattle and imagined my sibling transitioning now. I moved beyond wishing they would do it for my child to wanting my sibling to be happy. And they were, while we sat on the lawn.

Then Alex considered the life they had built.

"Maybe when I retire," they said.

After Indigo came out as nonbinary in high school, my mother, Alex, and Alex's son were over one night for Jason's homemade pizza. Mom was eighty-two that year.

"Now tell me nonbinary again," Mom said, and Indigo skipped through cisgender, genderfluid, intersectionality, and gender assigned at birth. My mother nodded, but the language was too new.

"You can think about gender like this," I said, and I pulled over the notepad we kept on the counter. "Draw three vertical lines and label them female, nonbinary, and male."

"And nonbinary is?" asked my mother.

"Not male, not female," said my nephew.

"Or both," said Indigo.

"And you put an X on each of the lines, higher or lower to show how you see your gender." I marked an X at the top of the female line. "I'm a lot female." I moved to the male line and put my X toward the bottom. "I like to lead and that is stereotypically male, so I feel a little bit male. And I feel a little nonbinary because I want to wear a pretty dress while I pound my way through life."

"Okay, I'll try it," said my mother. She stared at the lines. "Well, I love baseball," she said. She paused at the female line and shook her head. In the end, she marked herself low on the female line and high on the male and nonbinary lines.

"I've never really been female," she said. "Isn't that interesting."

When Jason had the pizzas ready to slide into the backyard oven, he joined us and marked his gender lines with the rest of the family. None of us were 100 percent female or male.

"Nobody knew about this back then," said my mother.

The grand diversity of gender will be more familiar for children who grow up today. A camp counselor will use they/them pronouns. A classmate will transition in elementary school. At a summer barbecue, an older cousin will say, "People don't have to be boys or girls, Grandma."

Let us sit on the lawn and imagine a time when a child tells their parent, "I am trans." And their parent grew up in a world that made room for it, that helped them breathe it in. Let us sit on the lawn and listen to the parent say, "I thought so. How wonderful. Come here, baby."

THE TAR ROCKS

I shouldn't have been at Goleta Beach that day. Two days earlier, on the Monday after graduating high school, I was supposed to interview for a summer job. Instead of taking the bus to my interview, though, I had opened the phone book on my mother's desk and looked up the address for the Army's recruitment center.

In the movie *Private Benjamin,* which had come out a few months before, the main character, played by Goldie Hawn, felt trapped by her family and thought joining the Army would free her. If anyone had suggested I was imitating Goldie, I would have denied it—I already knew my escape route. I'd been saving for college since elementary school. In fact, before looking up the recruitment center's address, I had written a list of supplies I would need for my dorm room at Cal Poly at the end of August.

Since I was not copying *Private Benjamin,* I cannot explain why I twisted my long hair into a bun, dressed up in a turquoise skirt, crisp white blouse, and espadrilles, and took the Santa Barbara city bus downtown. It felt as though my body was not under my control.

I thought the Army recruiter would be in a dress uniform with those ribbon stripes across his chest, but he wore camouflage.

"Why do you want to enlist?" he asked.

"Dunno." I stared at the recruiter and waited for him to give me the answer.

He could have had me sign the papers—I was eighteen—but he said I should talk with my parents and come back the next day.

On Tuesday morning, I slept in and missed my appointment with the recruiter. When my mom got home from work that night, I was still in bed, feeling like a rebel. I knew she would complain about me lazing around and was prepared to argue: "You lie in bed whenever you can." Back then, I didn't know my mother had depression.

Mom knocked on my bedroom door, but instead of complaining, she tilted her head. Her beige pantyhose had a run at the ankle she had stopped with clear nail polish, and I couldn't believe she walked around like that.

"Are you sick?" she asked.

"No, I'm not sick." I wanted her to feel sorry for me, so I sighed and scooched up in bed. "I almost joined the Army."

I expected my mother to yell that I was starting college in the fall. Instead, she sat at the end of my bed and asked, "Do you want to join the Army?"

My mom, who is white, grew up in Ecuador. She was sent to the United States during her senior year of high school and never returned. When I was eighteen, I wanted to leave my home, and when she was eighteen, she had been torn from hers—which was sad, but it meant she didn't know how to give me the guidance I needed. She never had the chance to feel stuck.

"I don't know what I want," I said. I only knew what I didn't: the unhappiness in our home, with Dad exploding, sisters whining, and Mom taking to her bed—all of them stifling my freedom. The end of August was too far away.

Mom rubbed my foot through the blanket. "Take a few days and go to the beach," she said. "You need sunshine." That was her cure if I had a cold or was grumpy or bored. Or almost joined the Army.

"I need to get a job," I said. She knew that. When I was ten, she told me, "You need to save for college," and hired me out as a babysitter for twenty-five cents an hour.

But now she said, "It can wait a few days," and patted my foot and went to make dinner.

Most of my friends had jobs that summer, but one girl, Diane, had just finished junior high and was too young for anything but babysitting. And she had a boogie board.

I called her after dinner. "Do you want to go to Goleta Beach tomorrow?"

I didn't know her well. She was fifteen, the age of my next-youngest sister, so I hoped she wouldn't be annoying. Although maybe I chose a younger friend so I could be the grown-up.

On Wednesday morning, Diane arrived at my house on her bike with her Styrofoam boogie board under her arm.

"You got your braces off," I said. I was surprised we were the same height. Her hair was halfway down her back, like mine, but darker blonde and wavy.

I grabbed the board I shared with my sisters, and Diane and I rode the three-mile trail to the beach. We locked our bikes next to the snack shop that hid behind the restaurant. "Sodas! Candy! Live worms!" read the battered chalkboard.

Ahead of us was the pier, where years before I had held my baby sister's hand so I could walk her to the end. She was scared of the water, though, and wanted me to carry her.

"I made us a peanut butter sandwich?" Diane's voice asked for my approval, so I smiled and said that was great. She took our lunch out of her backpack, and we stuffed in our shirts, shorts, and flip-flops before laying the sandwich on top.

"We're both wearing pink," Diane said, although her bikini was pastel and mine was magenta. I wore my second favorite swimsuit to the beach and saved my best for swimming pools.

It was morning-hazy over the water and the Channel Islands wouldn't be visible for a few hours. We carried our boards and beach towels and walked barefoot across the still-cool sand until we reached the shoreline, then turned right. The UC Santa Barbara campus squatted on the sandstone bluffs ahead of us, and the bluffs rounded the beach to point west toward the Pacific. At the end, they swelled out in two gentle curves, like the bosoms of a mermaid figurehead on the bow of a ship.

Once upon a time, the western end of the bluffs probably eroded to a single point. Over centuries, winter storms pummeled the point and formed the cleft in the mermaid's chest. Sandy-yellow boulders bigger than school buses fell to the ground, parking themselves half in the water and half on the beach, destined to slowly melt into the sand.

Gradually, the rocks turned black from oil that bubbled up from deep within the Santa Barbara Channel. The oil congealed into balls of tar, and currents pushed them toward the bluffs. For thousands of years, the Chumash people have used this tar to seal their baskets and canoes. Did the oil smother the rocks or protect them? Either way, the boulders became more tar than sediment. They became the tar rocks of my childhood.

When Diane and I trekked far enough from the families with shrieking children, we dug a hole in the sand, hid the backpack, and laid our towels side by side. We spent the day in the water, and Diane kept up with me, or maybe I kept up with her.

When we tired of riding to shore on the waves, we paddled out to the nearest buoy and sat on our boogie boards. Giant kelp reached from below to tickle our legs.

"When are you leaving for college?" Diane asked.

"Actually, I almost joined the Army." I told her about my Monday adventure and watched a line deepen between her eyes.

"Don't worry," I said. "I just wanted to get away."

"But the Army?"

I laughed, and she joined me. Only two days had passed and I already realized a signature could have swallowed me.

"Won't you miss it here?" asked Diane. She spread her arms wide to hand me the sea and sky.

"I want more."

"More than the ocean?"

I didn't know how to answer. My shoulders warmed in the sun, but my legs were cold where the waves gathered beneath me, lifting and letting go.

We balanced on our boards while a wave rolled underneath. It wasn't a big wave—for those, we held on to the metal handle of the buoy so we could keep talking.

It turned out both our moms were immigrants. Diane's mother was Greek and spoke that language on the phone with her sister, the way my mother spoke Spanish with her friends from the boarding school in Quito. Each of our moms married an American man, and each of those men was unable to love in the small, small ways our mothers wished for and needed. Diane and I wanted more than the lives of our mothers.

"My mom has no idea how to be American," I said, pulling seaweed onto my board and popping the bulbs.

"I know," said Diane. "My mom wanted me to wear a one-piece."

My mother didn't care if I wore a bikini at the beach—she learned early on that clothing changes with the environment. In the Ecuadorian rainforest, the Indigenous women who were her caretakers wore white blouses when they worked inside her parents' house. A mile away, in their Kichwa village, they switched to colorful fabric. Many of the children ran naked, and when my mother visited her caretakers' homes, she would strip off her romper and run around in her *bragas*.

When she was seven, Mom was sent to the mission school in

Quito, where clothing was required to be gender conforming and neatly ironed. When she moved to Minnesota to finish high school, the church did not allow her female Scandinavian relatives to layer pants under their dresses, not even to walk through a blizzard. And here, in sunny California, on the hottest Sundays, the women at our family's conservative church were allowed to forgo pantyhose.

My mom never objected to my sisters and me wearing bikinis at the beach in Santa Barbara. Clothing should adapt to the place where you live.

When Diane's and my shadows began pointing away from the ocean, we walked back to our towels to eat lunch.

"Ew, I stepped on a tar ball," Diane said, and I waited while she scraped her foot against a piece of driftwood.

Some people don't like the Santa Barbara beaches because of the dark flecks that stick to their swimsuits and the black crust that coats their feet at the end of the day. It is easy to step over the tar balls, though—golf ball-size, football-size, and bigger, flattened by the heat of the sun. Most of the tar that stuck to my feet came from specks too small to avoid.

Tar was a natural part of the beach, the adults around us said, harmless and easy to wash away.

Diane and I sat cross-legged on our towels and passed the sandwich back and forth. She surprised me by talking as fast and laughing as loud as me.

We discovered we both liked to bodysurf. After licking sun-melted peanut butter from our fingers, we left the boogie boards on our towels to swim beyond the buoys. Bodysurfing started where the larger waves began to swell. We counted for the seventh one, which everyone knew was the biggest, and rode it in until our limbs scraped against the sand.

With nothing beneath me, my body felt everything: cold water pushing me forward while I tried to hold my head above; the sun too bright when I blinked salt water out of my eyes; and, at the end of the ride, the rasp of sand against my stomach, arms, and thighs. My sisters never wanted to ride the waves without a boogie board holding them up. They hated the salt water stinging their eyes, even though the sensation lasted only a second. They didn't like getting water up their noses or sand in their suits, but I could ignore those small irritations. I would have bodysurfed naked if it were legal.

On our third ride, a breaker pushed me sideways and I rolled underneath, held down on the ocean floor by the churning surf. Sand and broken shells scraped against my back while the weight of the water rolled over me. The next wave filled my mouth with salt water, bitter from the flecks of tar. In between waves, the tide sucked me down, and I lay under the water with my eyes open, watched the brightness above, and wondered if I would ever rise back up to it.

I savored the precariousness. I knew about Joni Eareckson, who broke her neck when she dove into the water. My mother collected books about Christians who found hope within terrible circumstances. She made me read Joni's book when I was in high school: Look how faith can set us free! I was seventeen when I read the story, the same age as Joni when she became a quadriplegic. I remember thinking we both were confined, her by her body and me by my home.

And then the tide retreated, and the ocean let me go. I knelt in the softness of the after-wave, swung ropes of hair over my head so I could see, looked for Diane, and laughed because the sea gods had not captured me. You can't bodysurf without sometimes going under.

That evening, still in my bikini, I perched on the edge of the tub and used a hard brush and baby oil to scrub tar from the soles of my feet. The bathroom filled with a burnt-sugar scent like sweet poison, which to me was the smell of a day at the beach. When I washed the black slurry down the drain, my feet looked pink and innocent.

Diane and I rode back to the beach that Thursday and Friday. By the next week, I had a job, but on my days off, all summer long, we rode our bikes to Goleta Beach. Each of us taped a quarter under our bike seat so we could share a fifty-cent frozen Three Musketeers bar from the snack shop for our lunch.

We were muscular girls. I did gymnastics, and Diane was a runner. "B to the fifth" we called ourselves: big, blonde, buff, beautiful, and bitchin'. She told me a boy called her Thunder Thighs, and I said a boy called me that, too, and we smiled. Stupid boys.

Diane and I weighed about the same, although she grew taller than me that summer. American moms might have urged us to diet, but our mothers were immigrants. My mom said, "Finish your plate." She made two trays of enchiladas so my sisters and I could have seconds and thirds. When I ate a whole papaya at breakfast one time, she didn't complain.

Diane's mom made baklava. When I rode my bike to their house after work one Saturday, she handed me a thick, sticky-with-honey slice on a floral dessert plate.

"σκύψει," she said, which sounded like "Skeepsee." I thought it meant, "Eat up," but it really meant, "Keep your chin over the plate so you don't spill the crumbs."

I forget if I worked at the dry cleaners or the clothing store that summer, but when I got off work, if I wasn't babysitting, I either biked over to Diane's or went out with our group of friends. I made the boys who picked me up—those harmless boys with harmless crushes—also get Diane before we swam in someone's pool or went to a movie. It was 1981; we saw *Raiders of the Lost Ark* three times.

"My mom likes you," Diane said. "She never let me go out at night before."

My mom said I had to eat dinner at home once a week. I didn't dislike my little sisters—they were simply part of the family I wanted to escape. They still called out to our mom: Look what I made! Can you find my rainbow shorts? My older sister was home that summer, too, but she chose to live in the garden shed. Our mother wanted us to eat together once a week as a family, and although I am sure I complained, I understood she wanted us to feel loved.

One morning at the end of June, we saw a lemon bobbing in the water, and Diane ran out to grab it. We tore it in half with our fingernails and squeezed the juice and pulp onto our hair because we wanted our hair to be blonder. Since we wanted to keep the dried pulp on our hair as long as possible, we bought a frozen candy bar, walked to the end of Goleta Pier, leaned against the wooden rail, and stared across the water at the Channel Islands. I suppose Goleta Beach was beautiful, but that was unimportant to me. I wanted the scratch of the sand, the cold of the waves, and the hours away from adults.

"My dad's out there," Diane said. Both of us had angry dads, but I liked hers, who gave me hugs when I visited. Diane liked mine, who left us alone.

Her dad had been a fisherman. Before he got married, he saved enough money to buy his own boat. In 1969, though, when Diane was a toddler, he had to switch to ferrying supplies out to the oil rigs.

That winter, a few miles out from the Santa Barbara coastline, workers on Platform A finished drilling a borehole and pulled out the bit. Oil exploded out of the well. Union Oil tried to contain both the spill and the publicity, but a Coast Guard helicopter spotted the slick extending miles across the ocean.

Four million gallons of oil poured out. Thousands of birds and marine animals died. A dolphin washed up on the beach with its blowhole clogged with oil. Commercial fishing in the Santa Barbara Channel halted for more than a year.

Although the well was finally plugged, Platform A remained in the water off the coast of Santa Barbara. Within a few years of the spill, mussels and crabs, rockfish and corals began creating an ecosystem around its metal legs.

Diane said her dad always waited until he finished his supply trips for the day before he started drinking.

Another day at the beach, the morning haze burned off, coloring the water blue. The sand grew hot, so Diane and I put on our flip-flops and walked through the parking lot on our way to the snack shop. A guy putting a surfboard into his hatchback called out to us.

"Yeow, pretty girls."

We kept walking. The guy was barefoot, and I didn't hear him run up behind us. He tapped me on the shoulder, and I turned, standing in front of Diane as though she were my little sister. The surfer dude wore a big smile, freckles, and curly red hair past his shoulders.

"Wanna fuck?" he asked.

"No, thanks," I said, but I smiled as though it were a pleasant invitation.

He said, "Cool," and turned away.

Diane and I kept walking, and I heard her whisper, "Shit."

"That was nothing," I said. "That was easy."

I told her about the manager at my first real job, two years earlier, where the freezer was in the basement. How, when we needed more frozen fries, I begged the guys I worked with to go get them, but the manager said it was my job. How he followed me down the stairs and waited.

"On my way back up, he would say, 'A pass for a pass, blondie,' and grab my butt," I told Diane. "Every damn time."

"Shit," said Diane.

A few years before that, I had asked my mom what I should do when guys whistled and called out to me when I walked home from school.

"I don't know," she said. She had never been an American teen. When she was my age, she only walked around Quito in a group of students supervised by a missionary teacher.

I didn't bother asking my mother what to do about the fast-food manager. Mom wouldn't have had an answer, except maybe to say I should be more careful. In junior high, they gathered the female students in the auditorium to watch a video, scene after scene of girls being attacked because they didn't follow the rules—what to wear, where to walk, and why we should be at home when the sun went down at night—as though wearing a one-piece would protect us, as though nothing bad could happen in the daylight.

Over the years, I had used trial and error to figure out what to do about those yelling, whistling men, and now I taught Diane. In a public space, like a parking lot where other people were around, she should ignore a quick whistle or "Hey, baby." It usually stopped after that, but if the guy kept bugging Diane, she should pretend there was a reason she didn't hear him. If we were together, we could talk to each other and laugh. If she was alone, she could pretend her arm itched and start scratching it.

"That gives him a reason to not get mad," I said. "Maybe he'll stop hounding you."

"Why do they get mad?" asked Diane.

"I dunno," I said. "Sometimes they just do."

If the guy started following her, she needed to make him not feel bad. "I usually turn around and say, 'Hey, thanks!' and then I keep walking," I told her.

If he called her a bitch, she should run toward the nearest family. "You'll hear him laughing behind you, and it'll piss you off, but he won't follow."

How strange that I told Diane to run toward family, when all summer I wanted to run from mine. And how inadequate was my advice—yet does anyone know how to keep men from thinking they own the girls they see?

"What's in your backpack?" I called out to Diane while we rode to the beach, midway through the summer. She was ahead of me on the bike trail.

Looking back at me, she laughed and said, "It's a surprise."

After we set up our towels, Diane pulled out little kids' plastic pails and shovels. She also had a transistor radio. The music was staticky, but we sang along to Queen's "Crazy Little Thing Called Love" and the Go-Go's "Our Lips Are Sealed." We spent the morning building our castle in the sand, protecting it with a moat and decorating it with shells and seaweed before the tide broke through.

We hadn't visited the tar rocks in more than a week, and after our Three Musketeers lunch, we walked out to the western point. Low tide had uncovered the tidepools, which nestled among the rocks that were closest to the shore. Sea stars, mussels, green anemones, and clicking barnacles built their homes there, transforming what had been ooze into beauty.

Before we climbed onto a tar rock, we headed to one of the larger pools. A bright orange sea star was close to the edge. A breeze blew around the tar rocks, and when it created a miniature wave in the pool, a few of the sea star's legs breached the surface. Diane and I took turns running a finger across the marine creature's spiny back.

We had a favorite tar rock. Not one of the rocks that sloped so gently from the sand that even kids could scramble up. And not one of the farthest ones, where the tail ends of giant waves—the ones surfers liked to ride—crashed over from both directions.

Our rock was in the middle. Although the tide was low, we had to wait until the waves receded before running through knee-high water to reach the lowest foothold.

We walked to the end of our rock and stared across the sea. Waves hit the hardened wall of tar below us, and the seventh waves splashed gently on our toes.

"Who do you like?" Diane called out.

"I don't want a boyfriend before I'm in college," I said, loud enough that she could hear me above the waves. "I don't want to get stuck in Santa Barbara."

I listed the girls I knew who got pregnant: the middle school friend, the neighbor next door, the girl at my mom's church who now lived with her eighteen-year-old husband in a trailer behind a gas station.

"Do you like anyone?" I asked.

Diane said she liked Ricky, a boy in our friend group. He went to her family's church, where some of the women covered their hair with scarves as a sign of submission.

"My parents won't let me go to college," she said, "but I can get married after high school." That would be her escape.

We walked back to the center of the rock, where a patch of sand made a cushion for us to sit on while we analyzed the boys at her church. Who was the least like her dad? In the end, I agreed it was Ricky.

Later that week, I borrowed my mother's car and drove to Diane's house. I'd already eaten dinner, but her mom fixed me a heaping plate of moussaka, so I ate that, too.

Diane was excited about starting high school. We shared the chair at the desk in her bedroom while she showed me her stapled list of classes from San Marcos High, and I showed her my book of classes from Cal Poly. We both needed to choose our electives for the fall.

Her mom tapped on the doorframe. "I'm so glad you're helping Diane with this," she said.

"She's helping me, too."

She handed us a plate of baklava to share. After Diane chose choir for her elective and I had a list of first, second, and third choice classes for the fall, I carried the dirty plate to the kitchen. Diane's dad was watching TV, and I picked up his empty beer bottles on the way.

In the first week of August, I was in my bikini when Diane arrived at my house.

"Aren't you getting dressed?" she asked.

If my mother had been home, I would have put on my shorts and shirt for the ride to the beach. But Mom was at work.

"Nah, I'm good," I told Diane.

The bike trail followed the creek to Goleta Beach. Once we left my neighborhood, few people were on the trail and few catcalls came our way. Besides, the kind of men who called out to girls would do it anyway, no matter what I was wearing. I could make myself small with baggy clothes. I could wear a fast-food uniform—a polyester pantsuit, for god's sake. I could be in my church dress, and while everyone hugged the sign of peace, the youth pastor would say, "Peace of the Lord," and grind his hips against me. Riding in a bikini was a small rebellion, not like joining the Army would have been.

I wanted my freedom, but I didn't want to mess up my life. Small irritations, not fuck-ups. Tar without an oil spill; whistles without being grabbed. Being pushed down by a wave, yet rising to the surface.

The next time I had a day off work, Diane stripped off her shirt and shorts at my house and both of us bikini-rode to the beach. It was a Saturday and crowded with families, so we decided to walk to the tar rocks. We sang Bruce Springsteen's "Hungry Heart" while trudging through the sand.

Diane and I dropped our boards at the base of the cliff and checked above us. No one was there. The last time we climbed out on the tar rocks, a man in a windbreaker stood on the edge of the bluffs, watching us and jacking off.

When the water rushed out, we ran and climbed onto our favorite rock, not caring if we scratched our knees and palms. We wound our way past clusters of barnacles to the end of the rock where the waves crashed below us. Back then, we would have called it bitchin', standing on the edge of danger.

Diane yelled above the surf, "We'll be best friends 'til our boobs hang down to our knees!"

"To our knees," I yelled back.

Wind carried spray up to us, and it tasted salty.

"I'm leaving in ten days," I called.

"There's no such thing as ten days," Diane yelled. "In summer, all days are as one."

"Summer won't last forever."

"Yes, it will," she screamed into the wind.

Although I could not have named what I wanted, it was more than the freedom of the beach.

I riffed on the Springsteen lyrics we had sung on our way to the tar rocks. "Rip it apart, babe. You know it has to end."

Diane joined me while I finished singing the verse. We faced each other, spread our arms wide, and roared the "Hungry Heart" chorus.

We didn't see the giant wave until it crashed over and knocked us to the ground before sliding off the rock. We pushed ourselves to our knees and sat on the rough, hardened tar, laughing and whooping until the sun dried our skin.

After scouring my feet at home that night, I tried to scrub the tar stain from my suit, but I made a hole. A sacrifice to the gods of the sea. When I woke the next morning, my mom had left for work. The bikini, patched with a close-enough shade of pink, was folded neatly on my place mat.

Three weeks into August, with lemon bleached into my hair and money saved for college, I left for Cal Poly. It was a hundred miles up the highway and a million miles from home. Although I had wanted to scrape off my family, I came home on every school break the first couple of years.

Diane wrote me letters every week when I was away and signed them, "Love you 'til our boobs hang down to our knees." I wasn't as good at writing letters, but when I was in Santa Barbara, winter or summer, we rode our bikes to the beach.

My mother was right. I needed the beach. I thought I was stuck and couldn't have known that the summer I was eighteen was probably the freest I would ever be. Or I learned to create freedom within boundaries like a sea star at the tar rocks, to transform something unwanted into something beautiful, like my mother building a home in an unfamiliar land and making her daughters feel loved.

I remember feeling safe with my best friend by my side, both of us in pink bikinis, choosing to ignore the yelling, whistling men. I remember believing I could make up the rules for how to find the biggest wave and how to help Diane choose the boy she would marry.

Back then, I didn't realize there were beaches without tar. I thought the specks and tar balls were a natural part of the world, something to step around and—when I couldn't avoid them—to scrub off at the end of the day.

I AM THE DIPPY BIRD

My mother's face was often wet when I was young. Growing up in a missionary boarding school, then marrying my father, she had reasons to cry. She pretended not to be essentially a single parent, but sadness seeped into the Swedish work ethic she inherited from her parents: *Det är modet att fortsätta som räknas.* (It is the courage to keep working that counts.) My mother wept while fixing dinner after a long day at work and sobbed while hemming hand-me-down pants for her daughters. By middle school, I hated the dailiness of my mother's bawling. *Do something about it. Don't just cry,* I thought.

As free-flowing as she was with her tears, my mother did not want to see them in me. When I was grown and ran a preschool, and she worked as one of my teachers, more than once, she told this story to the parents who clustered at pick-up time: "When Ren was little and got cranky, I would tell her, 'Go to your room and come back when you have a smile on your face.' This one," my mother thumbed toward me, "never made it halfway down the hall. She would turn around with tears on her cheeks and say, 'I'm ready.' This one could make herself happy."

I don't remember standing in the hallway, yet I have almost always been able to choose happiness. Maybe I was a four-year-old in love with my mother and I dried up my tears for her. Just as likely, it wasn't her training, since my sisters were free with their tears.

However it happened, I grew to adulthood and rarely let myself cry. It's not that I don't feel sadness: When tears well up behind my eyes, I marinate in them before emerging into happiness again. Nature, nurture, or mind-body connection, it was a gift for me. Who wouldn't want to be happy?

In my thirties, Jason and I had a preemie, and Indigo had back-arching, red-screaming colic for five hours a day. My tears streamed out on those long afternoons. One evening, I heard Jason's key in the lock, so I wiped my face and swooped my infant up and down, giant swings over my head and under my legs to calm the screaming. By the time Jason walked into the kitchen, however, we were wailing baby and mama again.

One morning, in those early days of parenting, I heard Indigo crying and hurried down the hall. Jason had already picked up our newborn to rock and murmur. As I moved closer, I heard my husband whisper, "There's nothing to cry about, puppy."

I reached out and slid my arms under Indigo, pulled my baby to me, and turned away from my husband. "You can cry if you want to," I said.

Colic ended many months later, and soon after that, so did my tears. Did I use them all up, carrying my baby up and down the staircase, bouncing, bouncing, staring out the window?

My diagnosis was a fluke. When Indigo was in first grade, we went for a hike up Cougar Mountain, an hour east of Seattle. I scratched my eye on the branch of a tree, and the next day, the scratch had not healed. I saw an ophthalmologist, who noticed me sipping my water. After treating the scratch, he told me, "Your eyes are very dry. You should see a rheumatologist." He would not tell me why.

I searched online when I got home: "Very dry eyes, drinks lots of water." A trail of links led to a black-and-white photo of middle-aged Swedish women who wore dark glasses, carried jugs of water, and had a disease named after the doctor who discovered it. I read the description and thought, *that sounds awful.* Several weeks and lab tests later, a rheumatologist diagnosed my dry eyes, dry mouth, and arthritis; my balance issues and light sensitivity; the fatigue I thought was working-mama ordinary.

"You have Sjögren's syndrome," the doctor said without looking at me, as if she were telling the time. I wanted to argue it couldn't be true, but as quickly as my rage erupted, it disintegrated. My anger is locked up as well as my tears.

"Got it. Thank you," I told the doctor and took notes while she toppled my life.

Toward the end of our visit, with her back facing me while she wrote a prescription, the rheumatologist said, "Half of my Sjögren's patients use a wheelchair in five years."

I stared at the back of her white coat and breathed, breathed, before asking, "Do you think it will happen to me?"

"You should prepare for it," she said.

"Okay. Thank you."

When my sisters and I were young, our mother bought us a four-foot-tall inflatable clown. We punched the clown in the face, and it fell to the ground; then it bounced back up since the bottom was weighted. We were supposed to hit the clown instead of each other.

I am a bounce-up clown. I decided while on the exam bed, pressed down by the upcoming wheelchair, that however my Sjögren's unfolded, I would not let my sadness take over. A Swedish proverb says, "God gives every bird a worm, but he does not throw it into the nest." I would look for a way to be happy.

Back home from the rheumatologist's, while preventing my seven-year-old from bringing more caterpillars into our house, I wondered if I would have to close my preschool. I didn't want to walk away from what I had created. That evening, I shared my thinking with Jason, rat-a-tat-tat through the symptoms, the diagnosis, the lack of a cure. I mentioned the possible wheelchair.

"If it happens, we'll move to a place that isn't on a hillside. I'll want a snazzy-looking wheelchair, but they're probably expensive, so I can just yarn bomb the wheels."

Jason stayed quiet. He must have thought my temporary eye patch was the thing he had needed to worry about.

"The doctor said the best prevention is moderate exercise," I said. "She told me to walk every day, but dancing with the preschoolers is better than walking. If I keep my preschool going, maybe this Sjögren's will never progress."

Jason listened. He reached out to hold me. He did not tell me what he thought, but I already knew. I tend to believe what I want will come true, while he waits to see the evidence.

I understand my disability is strange. We call something strange when we cannot explain it. It is secretive, too, since four million Americans have Sjögren's, yet only a few times has someone heard of it when I have said its name. Many of us are white, cisgender female, diagnosed in our forties—like me. Our T cells squawk, "Foreigner! Foreigner!" at our lacrimal and salivary glands and muster our B cells to swarm and attack them. A rheumatologist told me Sjögren's emerges when genetics and hormones encounter a certain environment, but isn't that the definition of our lives?

Each of us with Sjögren's whips up our own ensemble of symptoms, our immunological self. We might need a sip of water to chew something sticky, like rice, or a mouthful of water to eat anything drier than soup. Our eyes might enjoy soothing drops once a week or burn with grittiness every hour of the day. Arthritis might visit one wrist, or we might not be able to walk.

For me, it's like being the Dippy Bird. When I was a child, a next-door neighbor had a toy, a mechanical bird with a top hat, a real feather for a tail, and a glass belly filled with red liquid. My neighbor would place a full cup of water by the toy and let me push down the red flannel beak so the bird could "drink." When I lifted my finger, the Dippy Bird's head would bounce up, but that wasn't the part that fascinated me: When the dampness on its beak evaporated, the bird would dip its head to drink again, forever and ever until the water ran out.

I don't know why I am so dry. I don't know what it means.

When we were young, my sisters and I had to memorize Bible verses, like this one from the book of Isaiah: "You shall be like a watered garden, like a spring of water, whose waters do not fail." I no longer believe in my mother's religion, but I would love to believe in that. I guzzle my water. I soak up my eye drops. I wish I had a natural spring inside me.

I grew up in California, where record-breaking drought has shriveled the rivers and lakes. (In Swedish, the *sjö* in Sjögren refers to a lake.) These days, I hear stories about the thirsty land from my friend Theresa, whose family has a ranch in central California. When we met in college, she told me, "We have water."

"Don't we all?" I asked, city slicker.

"We have well water," Theresa said.

When her ancestors bought the ranch, it came with rights to pump down to the Solano Subbasin, an unlimited water supply. Then came over-pumping, protecting the salmon, sales to bottled water companies, and decades of drought. Water no longer flows through irrigation ditches; now the family's land is dry farmed, which means they wait for rain to fall. The hydration you think will last forever sometimes can run dry.

For several years, Jason and I have visited a beach house on the peninsula, a ferry ride from Seattle across the Salish Sea. To build their house, the owners cleared land on a hill that was dripping with springs, but the construction triggered a landslide. Now the rivulets are diverted with rock walls and deep-rooted plantings. Water for the house comes from the largest spring at the top of the hill, water forever and ever.

After a family gathering there, one of my sisters said, "When the zombies roam the earth, we'll all head to that house," but I'd only been thinking about how green everything was on the hill.

One Friday night out on the peninsula, Jason and I went out for drinks, and a guy sitting next to us told us a tale about some loggers who found a pair of trees with branches twined around each other. (In Swedish, the *gren* in Sjögren refers to the branch of a tree.) When the loggers cut down the two trees, they found a small boulder the trees had been holding ten feet up in the air.

Jason and I are like those trees, but my branches hold Sjögren's directly, and his branches hold onto me.

My husband is used to embracing my strangeness, like the time arthritis seeped through my body. "Your whole body?" Jason asked. I slowly moved each joint and found one elbow did not hurt, so I focused on how good that elbow felt.

Another time, my lips swelled out more than an inch from my face, and Jason had to speed me to the hospital. Hoarse voice, shallow breath, I apologized for my monster face to the nurse who checked me in.

When the E.R. doctor learned I had Sjögren's, he told me I probably had a spontaneous allergic reaction. It could happen again, he said, "At any time, for no apparent reason."

Maybe I created my disease as a test for my husband: Do you really love me?

Because of the dryness in my nose, I have lost my sense of smell, which is a useful impairment when one works in a preschool. I can still taste food but not very well. Jason does most of the cooking, and he tells me the ingredients so I know which flavors I will taste. I miss the sensory input, so I stockpile other sensations. I turn up the music. I drag my shoes through gravel. I use a peppermint shampoo that tingles so strongly I think I can smell it.

I went to the national Sjögren's convention when it was held in Seattle in 2016. Several speakers said the syndrome might be triggered by environmental toxins, and I remembered the first time my body fought against me. For six months in my twenties, I lived in a town surrounded by farms that sprayed the air above their fields. Within weeks of moving there, I developed asthma and arthritis. A doctor told me pesticides may have been the catalyst, so I moved away and grew healthy again, except for the occasional need to lie down. Maybe Sjögren's is the languid unfolding of a poison, making me long for wetness.

I also learned at the convention that while patients can have any ethnicity or gender, my name and appearance might have hastened my diagnosis. Most Sjögren's patients struggle for years to learn what is wrong with their bodies. But the first time I showed a symptom to a doctor, I was told to see a rheumatologist. Was that a privilege of my Swedish name and yellow hair?

In 1930, ophthalmologist Henrik Sjögren examined a Swedish

woman with arthritis who sipped water constantly and had painfully dry eyes. Henrik presented her hodgepodge of symptoms to the leading eye doctors of Stockholm, but they saw nothing special, leaving him to figure it out on his own. Except he was not: His wife, Maria, was an ophthalmologist, too, and intertwined her research with his. She helped him locate and study nineteen more patients with the symptoms. Although Sjögren's syndrome has now been found in people all around the world—all ages, genders, and ethnicities—some doctors still think it is a Swedish disease.

Sjögren's patients generally don't make enough tears—in my case, not even a trickle. At the Sjögren's convention, I learned my lacrimal dysfunction is in the top 1 percent. I use artificial tears more than forty times a day. I can rip a vial off a five-pack and unscrew the plastic cap with one arthritic hand. I can squirt in eye drops while driving, both eyes open and watching the road. I know it is ill-mannered to use eye drops when in public, but if I were to leave the room each time my eyes grew scratchy-dry, I could never enjoy a conversation.

The dryness has damaged my eyes, of course: If you snap on a light, I will flinch. Jason sometimes hears me moan with pleasure when I put in my eye drops, but I try not to do that in public.

When I'm introduced to someone new, I tell them, "I have Sjögren's. My mouth doesn't make saliva, and my eyes don't make tears."

"I've never heard of it," the person will say. "What's it called again?"

"It's like *showgirls* and *Ren* . . . Sjögren's." I do jazz hands when I say this. Then I ask if it's okay to put in eye drops.

A panel at the convention discussed genetic risks, and on my padded conference chair, I dug my elbows into my knees, my fingertips into my forehead. Once in a while, Indigo asks me for eye drops, and my chest pinches tightly with fear. I tear off a plastic vial, hand it to my child, and try to sound nonchalant while I ask, "Are your eyes dry?"

"I just have something in my eye, Mom. Don't worry."

I dread that my dryness could flow to my child. Preemie-Indigo needed therapy for delays, and Rainbow-Indigo came out as queer in middle school. I know how to be a mama bear. I don't know how to wait.

In Swedish, *ren* as an adjective means pure, clean, and virtuous, as though I were destined to work with young children. My inability to cry does not fit with my profession. Preschool teachers are sensitive to children, sensitive to parents, sensitive. When I ran my preschool, parents and teachers were quick with their tears and their anger. I looked poised while they threw their voices at me, but my sadness was on hold. I must wait to feel big things until I am at home. I have learned how to cry without tears.

One morning, the husband of my best friend from childhood called me at work. Diane had entered hospice a few days before, a thousand miles away.

"She is finally at peace," her husband said.

I felt the grief grow behind my eyes, so I told my staff I needed to leave and called Jason to pick up our child from school. At home, I stripped off my clothes while climbing the stairs to our bathroom. I waited for the shower to warm to the temperature of tears before I stepped in, lifted my face, and let the falling water cry for me.

Sometimes a thing is so big I cannot hold it in until I reach the shower, and I let out a drippy-nose, hiccupping, high-pitched wail. When Jason hears me, he runs upstairs from his office and wraps his body around mine until I stop my shaking. He does not ask me questions, but I tell him anyway, word after word, until the big thing is small enough for us to hold.

A friend of mine at work said, "You must feel naked without your water bottle," and I laughed to make her feel good, but that's not what it's like. If my clothing fell off my body, I would feel embarrassed. If I don't have water near me, I feel like I could die.

In fact, my water bottle is covered by the Americans with Disabilities Act. I could legally carry it through a TSA checkpoint, although I would not trust the blue-shirted agents to believe my laminated card. They would have to consult the ADA binder, and who knows where that is kept. Would they take away my bottle while they searched for it?

I rarely travel anymore, but when my little family used to navigate the checkpoint, I would chew a stick of Trident spearmint gum to stimulate saliva. I would leave a sip of water in my bottle before setting it in the plastic tub, and in the body scanner, I would hold an eye drop vial in my fist. Indigo knew to walk ahead of me through the scanner, ready to grab my bottle and pass it to me like a runner's baton. Jason would follow behind to push our luggage through.

I have learned that needing too much water seems offensive to some people. Years ago, when Marco Rubio gulped water as he gave the State of the Union response, a news anchor snickered, "Can't he finish his speech without guzzling?"

At the Sjögren's convention, the meeting rooms had water, but the pitchers and glasses had been placed at the back instead of on our tables. Even the conference organizers did not realize what we needed, and when my water ran out in the middle of someone's talk, I had to snake between the tables to reach the oasis. It felt like a walk of shame.

I never told my preschoolers about my disability, but every year, at least one child would sense I needed water. One morning, while reading a picture book, I reached behind me for my bottle, but it wasn't there. It was someplace in the room, so I shouldn't have felt afraid, yet one of my preschoolers responded to the change in my voice.

"I'll look for it, Miss Ren," three-year-old Rafe called out. He jumped up from the circle rug and was back with my bottle before my mouth grew dry.

Indigo was like that, having grown up with my Sjögren's before we knew I had it. Sometimes I would lie on the couch for hours, choosing to not think about the fact that I would go, go, go, and then I would crash. I didn't know I had diagnosable fatigue—aren't all parents tired?

Baby-Indigo crawled and brought me board books to read, and Toddler-Indigo learned to refill my water bottle. When Indigo was seven and I spent a weekend in bed, my kid surprised me by doing the laundry, although the folding was atrocious. Years earlier, in my pregnancy class, while talking about our parenting goals, I had said I wanted my child to be kind. Having a disability is a handy way to raise an empathetic child.

When Indigo was two, we visited Santa's reindeer at Cougar Mountain Zoo. (In Swedish, *ren* means reindeer when used as a noun.) Jason and I showed our toddler how to let the reindeer nibble pellets we had bought from the dispenser. When the reindeer didn't notice little Indigo, I held onto the fence for balance and lifted my child, who had learned to not swing out too far from my body or I could fall over.

"We're helping Santa," I told Indigo.

By the age of three, my child knew that when we went for a walk, we needed to stop at curbs so I could ease myself down to the street. After Indigo grew big enough to help me with my balance, my child never stepped off a sidewalk without reaching back a hand toward me, as though asking for this dance.

For Indigo, my Sjögren's is a mother tongue, while for Jason the language was acquired in adulthood. If we are not already holding hands, my husband will step off a curb and walk a few paces, then remember and head back to where I teeter on the edge of the six-inch cliff.

When Indigo started middle school, I expanded my early childhood center. One Saturday morning, after moving to a larger facility, I was unpacking boxes while a troop of Boy Scouts volunteered outside. Unable to leave until the Scouts finished, by two o'clock I was crawling through the building, dragging the boxes behind me. My bones hurt. My fingers and wrists were swollen, so I used my hands like paws. I knew I should stop, and my body did it for me in the hallway, where I lay for an hour on the laminated floor.

A bigger preschool meant more parents, more employees, many more issues to solve. I no longer had time to dance with the children. Every morning when I woke, I lay in bed and felt my body. Was it a pain day? Could I move? Within a year of expanding the preschool, if I tried to walk for half an hour, I spent the rest of the day in bed. My rheumatologist said I should go on disability, but I didn't feel I had the right to leave what I had built. When Sjögren's could have cushioned my life, I stubbornly chose to not use it.

I decided if I wasn't going to let myself stop working, at least I would find a way to make my body move. I began leaving work with enough time to walk a few blocks in the afternoon, and within a few months, I could stroll for an hour. I didn't leave the preschool for several more years, but I slowly set boundaries, more and more until I finally said goodbye.

Now I take tromps around Seattle, and Jason usually comes with me. We have walked from our home in Capitol Hill two or three miles to the Space Needle, to Pike's Place, to Pioneer Square. If you don't know Seattle, that's mostly downhill. We stroll to restaurants and bars, dog parks and museums.

One afternoon, a few blocks from our home, a woman walking her dog called out to Jason and me. "You're the hand-holding couple! I've seen you walk past my house a bunch of times."

Would our hands have let go if I did not have Sjögren's?

I work part-time. I see my friends. I visit my mom at her memory care. Each month, she slips further into dementia, but her caretakers give her chocolates and hugs. During my visits, I write down her words to send to my sisters.

"I love that tree," she said one time. "It goes all the way up into the blue." Some things don't make sense, but we accept them anyway.

My mother remembers her early years but not the mission school. She remembers being a mother but not an unhappy wife. Besides *uff da*, said like a swear word, my mother long ago forgot any Swedish she learned as a child.

My mother no longer cries. A Swedish proverb says, *Ögon som inte gråter ser inte.* (Eyes that do not cry, do not see.) My mother has reversed the saying, in a way. Sometimes when I forget something, I think I will get Alzheimer's, too, and I wonder: If it freed my mother to be happy, will it liberate my tears?

I would not trade my happiness for tears. Maybe it is not a loss, my inability to cry. Maybe other people use their tears to keep themselves from feeling. And my experience with Sjögren's has not been as awful as it could have been. I am grateful I can walk. I am thankful for my eye drops and for Trident spearmint gum. I am amused that my penchant for happiness found its match in a disease.

But I wish I could cry tears of sadness. I wish I could cry tears of joy: tears for weddings and stomach-shaking humor; for Indigo's graduation and purple lupine on a hillside; for Ella Fitzgerald singing "Come Rain or Come Shine," and sappy TV commercials, and a friend's much-wanted pregnancy; for my husband's hand on the small of my back.

THE TARDIS IN OUR LIVING ROOM

On the BBC show Doctor Who, *the TARDIS is a sentient machine that travels through space and time. It looks like a London police box from the 1960s, but the TARDIS is a liminal space, transcending the world with which we are familiar.*

When I was pregnant with Indigo, my fifth graders made an illustrated book of baby advice for Jason and me.

"Be sure to take your kid to monster truck shows," Dustin wrote. "They're good for the whole family."

Jason and I, new to our marriage, laughed when we saw the ten-year-old's words. We are not monster truck people. Take away the trucks, though, and the advice is sound: Every family needs something to fascinate them.

The TARDIS is bigger on the inside. Characters on the BBC show tend to announce this after they walk through its navy blue doors. It takes more than one trip on the TARDIS, how-

ever, to realize the rooms and hallways can grow and adapt, depending on the journey. The TARDIS is a living labyrinth.

When Jason and I were dating, he referred to himself as a geek and I assured him, "No, you're not." But he did not see the word as a put-down: He thought being geeky was cool. Geeky people allow themselves to feel fascinated. Jason geeked out about coding software, welding sculptures, and perfecting his chocolate mousse.

After I left elementary school teaching and started my own preschool, an education journal arrived in the mail one afternoon. I clapped my hands when I saw it on the counter.

"Geeking out about early childhood," Jason said.

Over time, I adopted my husband's belief that being geeky is a good thing. I wanted to raise my child to be geeky. Geeky means you're curious. Geeky means you choose to be yourself.

Jason introduced Indigo to LEGO robotics when our child was four. Indigo wiggled too much to sit in a chair, so they moved everything to the basement carpet—laptop, wires, LEGOs, and wheels. After days of Daddy-kiddo time, they called me downstairs to watch them test their remote-controlled robot. Indigo in overalls and Jason in jeans, they leaned against each other on the floor, and their bangs touched while they whispered ideas about robot adjustments.

Jason is a geek who likes to work with his hands. When Indigo was six, my husband said, "Watch," and sliced the cord off a lamp. "We're going to rewire it," he told our child, and they did.

He bought Indigo a junior-size welder's helmet when our child was seven.

The summer Indigo turned eight, Jason started teaching our child trigonometry. "Just for fun," he said.

A week later, Indigo woke me at five thirty on a Saturday morning. "Is it too early to ask Daddy if we can do trig?"

I could have nudged Jason awake, but I am a kindhearted wife. "Wait until seven-oh-oh," I said, since the kid was learning trigonometry but could not read an analog clock.

Jason waited until Indigo was ten to introduce his favorite BBC science fiction show because, and I quote, "The concepts in *Doctor Who* are more complicated than trig."

> *"There's a lot of things you need to get across this universe: warp drive, wormhole refractors . . . You know the thing you need most of all? You need a hand to hold."*—The Doctor

Indigo was a happy little kid. When my friend Theresa flew up for a weekend and asked what she should bring my six-year-old for a birthday gift, I said, "Pick up a rock from your yard." My kid exclaimed over the rock, identified it as sedimentary, and made a pedestal for it out of wood scraps from the workshop Jason had built up the hill from our home.

When middle school arrived, however, Jason and I watched fear and sadness grow within our child.

"How can I help you?" I asked when Indigo made eye contact one day.

"You can't. They won't let me."

"Who won't let you, baby? What can't you do?" I asked, but my child stayed silent.

Many nights, after Indigo went to bed, Jason and I interrogated each other. Was this typical teenage angst? Were we being helicopter parents? Was our anxiety about our child's anxiety causing it? The danger signs parents are told to watch for did not exist. Indigo's long-time friend group was at our house as often as ever, teachers gave good reports, and our kid was more responsible with house chores than I was.

When the sadness continued, I made appointments for our seventh grader with therapists around Seattle, one after another, in search of someone my child would trust.

At the end of one session, a therapist whose white beard covered his chest like a bib pointed his index finger at Jason and me and said, "It helps teenagers to have regular family dinners."

"We do," Indigo said, rescuing us.

The therapist had no other suggestions.

At another clinic, the three of us squished together on a floral loveseat while the assistant conducting our intake asked Indigo about school. Trouble with teachers? Trouble with friends?

"I don't understand," she told our teen. She set her plastic clipboard on the side table with a thwack. "Why are you having a hard time if you have friends and you're getting all As?"

If I had stood up, Jason and Indigo would have followed me out of the office. But the assistant was the gatekeeper to the counselors at the clinic. What if a therapist hiding behind her clipboard was the one my baby needed?

When the TARDIS travels beyond 1960s London, it can use its perception filter like an invisibility cloak. Some people, however, can see the shimmer of the cloak and long to know what is hidden within.

In early October 2013, when Indigo was in eighth grade, our child called us to the red leather couch in the living room. The couch had white patches where our big dog, Toby, had licked away the color.

Indigo sat between Jason and me on the mostly red couch. The two of them waited while I lifted our little dog, Pugsley, onto my lap.

"Mom, Dad, I think I'm bisexual."

My husband and I nodded.

"I thought you'd have more of a reaction." Our fourteen-year-old's voice sounded like a complaint.

I remembered Toddler-Indigo, who had a different name back then, pointing to a different-colored box when I put pull-ups in our shopping cart at Target. Some boxes were pink with Minnie Mouse, and some were blue with Mickey. TV commercials insisted the padding location was geared toward pee hole placement, up or down, but I am a risk-taker. I pulled a second box off the shelf.

"You must have twins," the cashier said, stacking my pink and blue boxes.

I remembered Indigo refusing to queue in the boy line or girl line at preschool, so the teachers created an Indigo line. Indigo wanting nail polish with "short, short nails," and wanting a buzz cut, then wanting French braids.

When people asked me, "Do you have a son or a daughter?" neither answer felt correct. I figured my kid would be gay. I didn't know young children could be trans.

On the Toby-licked couch, I hugged my eighth grader. "I knew you were LGBT by the time you started kindergarten."

Indigo turned to Jason, who pretended to be shocked and said, "You're not straight?"

Our teen gave us a full-headed eye roll but laughed.

I ordered a bisexual pride flag with stripes of pink, purple, and blue and displayed it in our living room. Although I hoped coming out to us would solve our child's sadness, the flag was not enough. I had known how to help Indigo be happy at age six, but I could no longer see inside my child.

> *The TARDIS has a translation circuit, a telepathic field that allows beings—human or not—to understand each other's languages.*

In late October, both of Indigo's pupils dilated wide enough to swallow the irises. We drove to the emergency room, where the physician ordered a tox screen, a head CT, and an EKG, yet was unable to diagnose the black holes. Hours later, the pupils shrank.

That Monday, I could barely write a list of topics for the afternoon staff meeting at my preschool. We met in the art studio and pushed the children's tables together. The teachers scrunched around me on little rainbow chairs while I stared at my list, unable to corral their voices.

"What's with you today, Ren?" asked someone at the far end of the room.

I lowered my forehead to the table. The chatting and chair-shuffling halted.

I pushed out the words: "Something is going on with Indigo, and we don't know what it is." I told them about our family's trip to the E.R.

When I looked up, the teacher across from me had tears on her lower eyelashes. Many of my employees had known Indigo for years. When schools were closed, we brought our children to work, and the preschoolers followed our big kids around like groupies.

"What do you need from us?" asked Erica, who had worked with me for years.

"I don't know."

"What would make it easier?" asked another teacher.

Their gentleness gave me permission to ask: "Is there any way I could take a day off each week until we know what's going on with Indigo?"

If I had said I needed an extra sentence from each of them for the weekly newsletter, my staff would have protested, but for my child, they were eager. Take the time Indigo needs, they said. They would handle the broken copy machine and the parent at pick-up time who had an overabundance of questions.

Indigo's pupils never dilated like that again. Jason and I decided it must have been anxiety.

> *Serious* Doctor Who *fans—they call themselves Whovians—like to speculate about TARDIS anomalies. They use phrases like "dimensional threshold" and "atmospheric excitation." They debate online whether a part detached from the TARDIS could be used as a stand-alone bridge between space and time.*

At the end of November, Jason called me at work to say he wanted to show me something he'd built. Could I sneak over to the workshop without Indigo?

That afternoon, I stared at the enormous blue box in my husband's workshop. It was not giant enough, I would learn. A 1960s London police box was five feet wide and ten feet tall, but the ceiling of Jason's workshop was only eight feet.

"Most people don't realize how big a TARDIS is," Jason said. "It almost scared me off the project entirely."

He had to scale down the blueprints from www.tardisbuilders.com —although, Jason said, he did not want to shrink his creation too much. "If Indigo had to duck to walk through the doors, it would destroy the illusion that it was full-scale."

Jason said he trimmed the TARDIS to around 90 percent. Numerically, my husband tends to be more precise.

"Ninety-one percent?" I asked. "Eighty-nine?"

"Actually," Jason said, "it's thirteen-fifteenths scale."

My husband made a thirteen-fifteenths scale TARDIS and adapted every measurement for every board he cut.

"Of course, there are people online who take this very seriously," he said.

Jason said he wanted to give the TARDIS to Indigo for Christmas. I will translate for my husband, who creates instead of talking: He and Indigo spent hours watching *Doctor Who* together, so Jason built the TARDIS as a giant symbol of his love.

Since our family would host Christmas dinner and Jason would do most of the cooking, he planned to reconstruct the navy blue box at our home and present it to Indigo the day before.

"That's why I numbered every board."

"Good thinking," I said, but I wanted to know how a TARDIS would fit into our world.

"Is it going outside?" I asked. I stepped over scrap wood and circled the tower of blue.

"It won't hold up outdoors," Jason said. It rains too much in Seattle.

The TARDIS was too large to fit in Indigo's bedroom. The light for the top sat to the side, waiting for a bigger space. I understood the giant blue box would have to move into the living room. It would be a showboat of our geekiness. Our neighbors would laugh but not in a mean way. Indigo would love it. We would need to shift the couch.

Jason watched me, as eager as Toby when I clipped on the leash. I knew why he built the TARDIS without telling me—creativity is fragile—yet I needed a moment to process the change to our home. He looked down at the floor where the cracks between the boards were packed with sawdust, and I softened. I wanted to be the kind of person who celebrates her partner's art by inviting a TARDIS into her living room.

"If we move the yellow painting, it can go against that wall," I said.

The TARDIS generates enough oxygen to keep its passengers alive no matter where they travel. It can even project an air bubble beyond its walls. If, while traveling through outer space, people on the TARDIS want to open the double doors to get a better view, the TARDIS will protect them with a bubble.

To give Jason time to reassemble the TARDIS the day before Christmas in 2013, I drove our child and three middle-school friends to the movies. When Indigo and I returned home, Jason met us at the carport.

"Close your eyes," he said to Indigo, and they walked down the stairs to our hillside house with their arms around each other's shoulders. In the middle of the living room, my husband said, "Open your eyes."

"You made me a TARDIS!" shouted Indigo. Our dogs ran into the room, and their toenails clicked across the wood floor.

Jason pointed out the BBC-approved paint color; he explained that the phone box didn't open, just like a real TARDIS. He showed off the faux perception filter he had glued to the key, and Indigo took the key and unlocked the double doors. The two of them stepped inside, closed the doors, and disappeared, although I could hear them murmuring.

In the winter, Seattle nighttime falls midafternoon, and our living room windows were already black. I looked at the Santas lined up on the windowsill, out of Toby's tail-whacking reach, and at the Christmas tree with no ornaments on the bottom half so Pugsley wouldn't eat them. The light on top of the TARDIS was the brightest thing in the room. I heard Indigo whisper to Jason, "If I read a book in here, it would be bigger on the inside."

The next evening, after our dinner guests left, Indigo and I pulled a twin mattress down to Jason's basement office so we could watch the *Doctor Who* Christmas special. His office had flooded from a rainstorm the week before, and we had moved the furniture upstairs, ripped out the carpet, and set up the pump.

The movie screen Jason had long ago painted on the wall remained intact, so while he whacked together a stand for the projector, Indigo and I scooched the mattress against the wall and added pillows for our backs. A bubble of softness.

> Doctor Who *has run on the BBC from 1963 until today. In the 2013 Christmas special, "The Time of the Doctor," the Doctor loses his battle with the Daleks. Eleven million people in the United Kingdom and two million in the United States watched the universe crack itself open so the Doctor could be reborn as a new man—and a new actor—to keep the TV series going. (A few years later, after regenerating as a man for half a century, the Doctor would emerge as a woman.)*

The morning after Christmas, Jason and I read our new books on the couch. Our legs overlapped, and I sipped cinnamon tea for my cold while the TARDIS watched over us. Acoustic guitar from our holiday playlist lingered in the air, and our dogs snoozed, almost touching, in front of the sliding glass doors. The gray of Seattle hovered outside the glass.

Our child hovered, too, waiting for me to emerge from the words in my book and nudge Jason with my knee.

"Mom, Dad, I need to tell you something."

We lowered our legs, and our teenager slid in for a moment, then pushed off the couch and moved to the daybed across from us. Jason grabbed my hand. Minutes passed. I watched our child breathe. My husband had no need to fill the silence, and to stop myself from talking, I pushed my fingertips under my thighs.

I could not stay quiet forever. "We love you. You can tell us anything."

The TARDIS waited with us.

Finally, Indigo spoke the words. "I'm transgender."

It was not a bombshell for me, more of a sparkler, a shimmering flame I could hold in my hand. Even so, seconds passed before I rose from the couch, crossed to the daybed, and scooped my baby to my body. Jason followed, and we made an Indigo sandwich.

The dogs woke up and padded toward us. Pugsley scratched the daybed, but I did not lift her up. In the air, a Spanish guitar strummed "Silent Night."

With his dark hair pressed against our child's light brown, Jason whispered, "We love you."

> *During World War II, the Germans dropped more than two thousand bombs on Wales, which terrified a little boy named Terry Nation. Two decades later, as a screenwriter for* Doctor Who, *Nation created the Daleks. He based them on the Nazis. In the show, Daleks are engineered to never feel kindness or empathy, only hate and fear. They view all other species as inferior and seek to kill anyone who refuses to conform to their rules. "Exterminate!" the Daleks chant.*

I was raised in a society that believed in only two genders, which were easily differentiated at birth by glancing between an infant's legs. Humans have not always believed this, not all around the world, not throughout history. The TARDIS entered my living room, and soon a world hidden from me grew big enough for me to see.

I would learn that *hijras* (third-gender people) have lived openly in communities for thousands of years in India. And that in the 1500s, in what is now called South America, Spanish colonizers wrote in their journals about *mujerados* (rough translation: male women). And that when industrialization herded people into US cities in the mid-1800s, gender diverse people found each other and began revealing what they had tried to keep hidden on the farm.

I would learn that European colonizers, and US states and cities, sought to eliminate gender diversity by legal and violent means. Also, that the laws they wrote to force people to conform ipso facto proved the existence of gender diversity.

TARDIS, n. — *First published in the* Oxford English Dictionary *in 2002*
Transgender, adj. and n. — *First published in the* Oxford English Dictionary *in 2003*

Still on the daybed, now holding our laptops, Jason, Indigo, and I researched how to help a transgender teen. The hate online was inescapable. Transgender adults recounted suicide attempts and losing jobs. Parents of trans children described being yelled at by neighbors and having their kids bullied at school.

The sky outside grew dark, and we closed our laptops. Indigo and Jason began analyzing yesterday's *Doctor Who* Christmas episode.

I lifted Pugsley off my lap, not knowing how she got there, and went upstairs to the shelf where we kept office supplies. I needed a binder and tabs. I did not know all the steps for my new project, but I knew my goals: to find out how to help my child transition and to make our world ready for Indigo.

When Indigo went to bed that night, I attempted to tuck in my fourteen-year-old but was rebuffed. My head-clogging cold wanted me to go to bed, too. Instead, I trudged down to Jason's basement office, where he had set up a folding table for his computer. He stared at the monitor while I slumped to the twin mattress on the floor.

"This is big," I said.

Jason left his computer and lay down on the mattress with me and my tissues.

"Are the neighbors going to firebomb us?" I asked.

"Probably not," he said.

"What will we do if it isn't safe?"

"I've been looking at jobs and housing in Oregon."

"It's good, though, right?" I asked. I was starting to see my child's gender as expansive, not only for Indigo but for me.

Jason nodded, and we lay there, listening to the rain.

> *The Doctor owns a handy sonic screwdriver. Beyond attaching one object to another, a sonic screwdriver can change the nature of atoms. It can amplify, build, camouflage, download, eject, force, geolocate, hack, ignite, jam, kill, loosen, manipulate, navigate, open, pressure, quash, radiate, scan, teleport, unlock, vanish, wobble, x-ray, yank, and zap.*

I started a checklist on the first page of the binder, and it went on for many pages. Some tasks would be drudgery, some a delight. My checklist, I hoped, would change the nature of the story.

"Your whole family is on a journey," Aidan Key, the founder of Gender Diversity, told me over the phone the morning after Indigo came out as trans. He said people often wrote a letter to inform their friends and family, and I thought of my weekly newsletters at preschool, how the parents liked stories and pictures of their kids.

Within days, I had designed a colorful booklet that overflowed with stories and photos. Indigo as a baby, toddler, little kid, now. You know our child, you love our child, Indigo could be your child, I wrote. Everything has changed, nothing has changed. I suppose I was inviting them to build their own TARDIS, to remember that as parents we try to enlarge our children's worlds. We don't always realize they will do the same for ours.

When Indigo was ready to come out publicly, I handed out the booklets. I held a brunch with girlfriends and a parent meeting at the middle school. Jason made his chocolate chip cookies, and we invited neighbors over. I told people we hadn't seen in years, anyone who could bump into my child and say the wrong name, the wrong pronoun. I believed if I told the story well enough, with adorable photos and warmth in my voice, most people would want to support my child.

It was 2013, only a decade ago, but a third of the people who read the booklet told me they had never heard the word transgender. Very few, however, refused to walk through the door to see the new world I described.

> *"We're all stories in the end. Just make it a good one, eh?"*
> —The Doctor

Sometimes, it was like a fairy tale.

Indigo had an orthodontist appointment at the end of January. The week before, checking an item off my list, I drove to Dr. Lake's office to change the name and gender marker on my child's records.

The transaction was matter-of-fact, as though the receptionist heard stories like ours every day. "Oh, I love the name Indigo," she said. "Let me get the file." Still, my hand shook when I handed her a booklet and asked her to share it with her coworkers and Dr. Lake.

I forgot to tell Indigo I updated their file. When we drove there the next week, my baby whispered, "How do I tell them?"

"I already did," I said, chipper-voiced to hide my worry.

In the entry to Dr. Lake's office, there was a computer where patients typed their first name to signal their arrival.

"Mama?" asked Indigo.

"Type 'I,'" I said, and Indigo's name popped up on the screen. My baby turned around and hugged me.

Still, when they called Indigo back for the checkup, I wished my child were younger so I could sit next to the dental chair. Fourteen-year-olds do not want their mothers hovering.

I did not pick up the *People* magazine on the side table. I stared straight ahead, mom-bag over my shoulder, hands clasped between my knees. Fifteen minutes later, Indigo walked toward me with one of Dr. Lake's assistants.

"Everything looks good," the assistant called to me.

In the car, before I started the engine, Indigo leaned toward me and said, "Mom, guess what? When Dr. Lake was looking at my braces, he grabbed my shoulder and said, 'I'm proud of you, kiddo.'"

> *"We're capable of the most incredible change. We can evolve while still staying true to who we are."*—The Doctor

A decade ago, the TARDIS moved into our living room, the way big things appear in our lives. What did it think of the world that transformed in our home?

Every family needs to move beyond the world with which we are familiar. When we build a TARDIS for our child or share our monster truck shows, we whisper to our children that they can be themselves.

In January 2014, Jason and I scanned the internet to learn how to help our child transition.

In February, Indigo came out at school. The eighth-grade class and a few trusted adults sat in a circle while our baby announced, "I'm transgender." Later that day, the eighth-grade advisor told me the middle schoolers stared at the ground, motionless and silent, until one of Indigo's best friends stood up.

"Big hug!" said the six-foot boy, crossing the circle to grab my child.

Indigo's group of friends stayed the same, switching to my child's new name and pronouns as easily as slipping off a coat when coming in from the rain. Being different on the inside was something they could easily imagine. They were at our house as often as before, asking for snacks and switching from talking to texting each other when I entered Indigo's bedroom with the requested chips and soda.

Seven middle schoolers, it turns out, can fit inside a thirteen-fifteenths scale TARDIS.

RESURRECTING MY MOTHER'S CHILDHOOD: A Thematic Analysis

"Of course, this goes back to the jungle."—Mom

ABSTRACT

Soon after Alzheimer's began to change my mother, as though a fairy had twinkled a wand, I realized she was happy. When we walked arm in arm, she sometimes took a little hop.

If you look up at the blue, you can hear the moon with me, she said while we strolled through the garden one day at her assisted-living center.[1]

I began scribbling her words in a spiral-bound notebook, typing them when I got home and emailing the transcript to my research team—by which I mean my sisters. At first, we mourned our mom's decline, but in our weekly Zooms over the last three years, Thora, Sigrid, Greta, and I have also reveled in our mother's newfound sense of wonder. Mom won a golden ticket in the Alzheimer's temperament lottery, yet it is more than that: Since we were young, my sisters and I have rarely seen our mother's joy.

[1] All italicized quotes are from the transcript of my mother's words.

When we were children, our mother laughed while telling us stories about growing up in the rainforest in Ecuador, where her Scandinavian parents were missionaries.[2] She called her childhood home "the jungle."

Mom remembered running barefoot outdoors as soon as morning prayers were over, playing among the trees, listening to the birds, and catching crabs in the river. She said llamas smelled musty and mangos smelled sweet, but she did not like the mangos that fell from the trees because they were stringy. It was better to climb up and choose the fruit she wanted to eat.

"Do you remember how she sounded?" I asked my sisters, and we wandered through our memories. Sigrid said our mother's voice sounded light because the jungle was where she was "innocent and unbroken."

A research question grew within me: Can Alzheimer's restore the felt sense of a person's early childhood?

INTRODUCTION

> *"Still stands the forest primeval; but far away from its shadow," wrote Henry Wadsworth Longfellow in his poem "Evangeline: A Tale of Acadie."*

Thematic analysis looks for patterns in people's words, and I had three years' worth of quotations to examine. Many daughters seek to understand their mothers, although fewer will color-code their mother's words and sort them into themes. I knew her words held knotted threads my research must untangle: religion and colonialism, depression and escape. Academic distance is useful for a researcher who wishes to explore her mother's jungle.

I focused on coding words instead of thinking about the day I

[2] When I was a child, I told people my grandparents were missionaries. In my teens, after learning missionaries were not benign, I started telling people my grandparents ran a school in Ecuador, which was true, though not the whole truth.

found my mom standing pale and naked in her assisted-living studio with her mouth gaping like a baby bird, and when I handed her a pull-up, she put it on her arm. Highlighting quotes in a rainbow of colors let me silence the memory of those months of lockdown—with visits through sliding glass doors that were locked. Mom could not remember to hold up the phone while she talked, so I pressed my ear against the crack between the doors to listen.

Alzheimer's disease makes a cognitive U-turn. Children advance through Jean Piaget's stages of development, and dementia rewinds along the same path. Piaget described children ages two through seven as being in the Preoperational Stage. They are inquisitive about the world and combine their observations with magical thinking.

My sisters and I observed our mother's downward spiral[3] while she reentered the Preoperational Stage. (See Figure 1.)

Fig. 1, Mom's cognitive decline

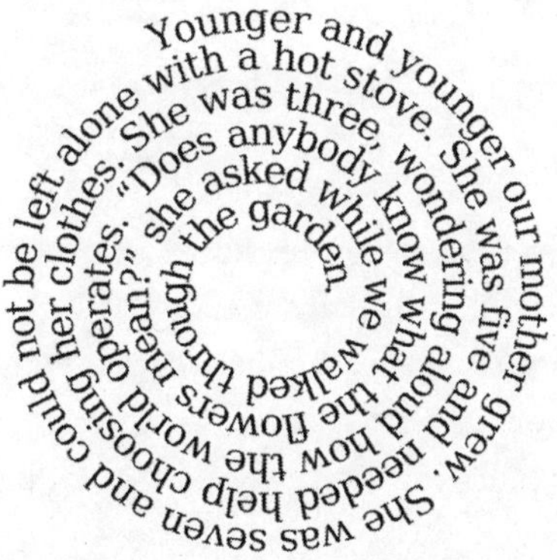

If my mother is rewinding, what will I find at the end of her path?

---

[3] My mother immigrated to the United States decades before deforestation in Ecuador uncovered petroglyph spirals that are thousands of years old. Western archeologists have yet to determine the meaning of the spirals. I do not know if they have consulted Indigenous Ecuadorians.

LITERATURE REVIEW

Reviewing literature is a way to procrastinate when one does not wish to think about what happened to one's mother. I read about Alzheimer's, Ecuador, and the people of the rainforest. That led to colonialism, Spanish explorers, and the Indigenous and European languages that surrounded my mom; to missionaries and mission boarding schools; to abuse.

I was not limited to books and websites. Few documents exist from Mom's childhood, but I also had my sisters and their memories.

"We're a hive," said Thora.

The most important literature for my review was our mother's words, which I followed as though they were the breadcrumbs in a fairy tale, slipping through a little girl's fingers while she walked deeper into the forest.

BACKGROUND

The neurologist who diagnosed our mom would have taken a medical history.

> Janet is an eighty-five-year-old white female residing in Seattle, Washington.
>
> Family: Divorced, four daughters
>
> Occupation: Retired teacher
>
> Birthplace: Riobamba, Ecuador

The doctor included cursory notes about our mother's childhood.

> Four months old: moved from Riobamba to a rainforest in northern Ecuador, where her parents founded a school for Indigenous boys
>
> Seven years old: sent to a missionary boarding school in Quito
>
> Late teens: when her father needed medical care, immigrated to Minnesota, where her family had Swedish relatives
>
> Never returned to Ecuador

Medical notes cannot fully record anyone's story. (See Figure 2.)

Fig. 2, Items the neurologist did not write in Mom's notes

- A few years after our mother immigrated to the US, she met our father at church in May and married him in August.
- Around the time I started kindergarten, our father told her to stop speaking Spanish with my sisters and me. One time, when I needed help with Spanish homework and asked why we did not speak it anymore, she said, "He didn't want you girls talking behind his back."
- In the early 1980s, our family's church joined the Sanctuary Movement to provide safe haven for Central American refugees. Mom signed up as a translator, but our father forbade that also.
- After divorcing our father, our mother taught Spanish-speaking migrant children in California. When three of her four daughters moved to Washington, she joined us in Seattle and directed the Refugee Language Institute until she retired.
- Now, when my mom helps to choose her own clothing, she loves to mix florals and stripes; now, her hair is soft and white and begs to be petted.

METHODOLOGY

I transcribed 250 pages of conversations with my mother when she was eighty-six to eighty-eight years old. This analysis covers conversations from March 2020 through December 2022. Mom lived in an assisted-living center for the first two years, then in a memory care unit, both in Seattle.

She knew I was recording her words and thought we were writing a book. One morning, while we sat in the garden, she tapped my notebook and said, *I have to do a little bit of writing to remember me what's happening.*

In addition to transcribing my mom's conversations with people, I recorded her chatting with stuffed animals and objects in nature (trees, flowers, etc.). She had a pet coat hanger for several months and carried it everywhere, but I did not hear her talk to the hanger.

I emailed Mom's quotations to my sisters in 132 weekly sections.

We read them aloud to our partners and children, whom I soon added to the email thread. Three women who considered our mom a second mother asked to join the list. Almost every week for three years, I emailed a transcript to a dozen people. I still do.

I hold my mother's legal power of attorney and give permission for her words to be used in this paper. My sisters approve, although unsurprisingly, they had opinions about which quotes I should use. The four of us (see Figure 3) conducted research, i.e., talked about our mom, during Sunday-night sister Zooms in January and February 2023.

Fig. 3, Our mother's daughters, oldest to youngest[4]

- Thora works in neurology at a hospital near Seattle, Washington.
- Ren, the author of this paper, ran an early childhood center and is now a parent educator in Seattle.
- Sigrid is a family practice physician serving Spanish-speaking migrant workers in central California.
- Greta works in pain management at a military clinic in southern Texas.

Mom no longer remembers the details in Figure 3. Most of the time, she does not remember she has four daughters. "You are my mother," I tell her at the start of every visit.

A sample of her responses:

You tell me that pretty regularly, but it moves to another spot.

And you're my brother or my sister or whatever.

Did they ever give a definition of my being your mother?

Line by line, through 250 pages, I sorted Mom's quotations into themes. When the entire document vibrated with blocks of color and was ready to analyze, I used a latent approach: digging beneath the words to search for underlying meaning. This approach is essential

[4] It is as though we designed our professions to someday research Alzheimer's, childhood, healing, and our mom.

with the text of an Alzheimer's patient whose ideas have a tendency to wander.

While conducting the thematic analysis, I realized postcolonial criticism, although not directly applicable because my mother is not an Indigenous person, could offer insight.[5]

RESULTS

Four paired themes emerged from the analysis:

1. Aphasia and a search for knowledge
2. Languages and other people's choices
3. Missionary school and colonialism
4. Depression and delight

Theme 1: Aphasia and a search for knowledge

I was born in Ecuador, and you would not have been with me in that particular situation.

QUANTIFICATION

Word loss is common with Alzheimer's patients. Each of the 132 weekly transcripts contained evidence of aphasia: *It was a refrigerator. Obviously, I don't mean refrigerator.*

Most of my mother's stumbles were with nouns, although nouns are not the important part of this story. Mom called the puzzle table *the table full of names*. She called her friend Betty Lou's walker *a wheelie cane*. When she could not remember the name for an object, she often described its use or what it felt like to her.

> The shower: *It's not a washing machine, but we can have our body fixed.*
>
> Rain: *It's the season of the time.*

[5] History belonging to the winners and all that, scholarly analysis has traditionally focused on the views of the colonizers. Postcolonial criticism tries to look through the eyes of those whose language, land, and culture were colonized.

One of her daughters: *I'm looking at somebody that would be a continuation of what I am.*

Less common in Alzheimer's patients was our mother's eloquence. Virtually every weekly transcript contained advanced vocabulary, as well as language that sounded insightful. Even her made-up words made sense.

Men-wise, I would say there are three men.

Hopefully, I'm helpfully.

Moreover, the entire document contained 224 questions that showed a sense of wonder.

What is the real story that is yours?

Do you have a tendency to be in that situation every day?

I'll probably live to one hundred. I hope I'm looking up at the sky. I wonder what our last conversation will be?

PATIENT HISTORY FOR THEME 1: APHASIA AND A SEARCH FOR KNOWLEDGE

Our mother taught high school English before having children. When I was in middle school and she couldn't drive me to a school event, instead of telling me to "find a ride," she said I needed to "pursue another avenue of transportation." Despite her expansive vocabulary, her conversations with my sisters and me remained surface-level.

"Mom never asked us deep questions," Thora said on a Sunday-night Zoom. "She probably didn't realize parents were supposed to give guidance. In her mind, you were supposed to pray about it."

"She let me talk about my concerns if I brought them up," said Greta, "but her advice was practical, not philosophical."

ANALYSIS OF THEME 1: APHASIA AND A SEARCH FOR KNOWLEDGE

Despite the occasional flubbed word, my mother's current speech is too complex to align with a standard stage of language development. Her aphasia also does not reflect how she talked in early childhood since she did not speak English then. Not everything goes back to the jungle.

But maybe her search for insight does. According to Piaget's child development theory, the Preoperational Stage, ages two through seven, is characterized by a curious mind. I wonder if, by lowering inhibitions, Alzheimer's can uncover a buried desire for knowledge. When my mother lived in the jungle, was she like Eve, seeking the fruit from every tree?

Growing up, the only time I encountered my mom's sense of wonder was when she talked about the jungle. What would my childhood have been like if she had asked me questions like, *What is the real story that is yours?*

Theme 2: Languages and other people's choices

Much of it would be easier if I could just say it in Spanish.

QUANTIFICATION

Although most of the words I recorded were in English, my mother spoke Spanish or expressed a desire to speak Spanish in 64 percent of the weekly transcripts. Examples:

> *¡Qué bueno, bueno, bueno!*
>
> *¿Qué recuerdo de Ecuador? [What do I remember about Ecuador?]*
>
> *The Spanish is as real to me as anything.*

PATIENT HISTORY FOR THEME 2: LANGUAGES AND OTHER PEOPLE'S CHOICES

English was not my mother's first language. Neither was Spanish. Her first language was Kichwa,[6] which was spoken by the Indigenous women who were her primary caregivers. Mom's baby book holds photographs of them. A Kichwa woman captioned "Rosa" holds my mother outside a wooden building. A Kichwa woman cap-

[6] Beginning in the 1500s, Spanish colonizers used the spelling "Quechua." Although several South American countries continue to spell it that way, Ecuadorian Kichwa does not include the letter Q.

tioned "Clotilde" holds my mother in her lap.[7] They called her Kinti, which means "hummingbird."

My youngest sister said that one afternoon in the memory care garden, our mom bent her knees, pointed to a bush, and said, *Sometimes I have to crawl under this one.* Greta wondered if Mom thought she was a child again, playing hide-and-seek with her Kichwa playmates. In the baby book, now almost ninety years old, our grandmother's cursive writing says, "She had many friends among the Indians in the jungle Oriente."[8]

When I was a child, my mother's jungle sounded like the Garden of Eden.

"She played with the Kichwa boys, climbing trees and swimming in the river," remembered Thora. "And there was something about her parents thinking she was lost and finding her in a field of flowers."

The rainforest was "where she had an original version of herself," said Sigrid.[9]

Our grandparents grew up speaking Swedish, Norwegian, and English. Their missionary group ordered them to move to Ecuador and learn Spanish so they could teach it to Kichwa boys. Despite not being fluent, our grandparents decided to mainly speak Spanish with their daughter, our mom. They did not speak Kichwa when they moved to the rainforest, although they recorded words and phrases in their notebooks. (See Figure 4.)

---

7 Rosa and Clotilde are not Kichwa names. It is likely the women were given those names by my grandparents or other Western missionaries.

8 Spanish colonizers named the Ecuadorian region east of the Andes *el Oriente* instead of using an Indigenous placename. They named the country Ecuador, the Spanish word for *equator*.

9 I heard an echo of my mother's stories in a video from the 2022 Bioneers Conference, when Kichwa Indigenous rights activist Helena Gualinga shared stories about her childhood in the Ecuadorian rainforest. "We grew up climbing in trees, swimming in the water," she said. Standing next to Helena on the stage, her sister, Nina, added, "The forest is our family."

Fig. 4, Kichwa-English mini lexicon[10]

KICHWA	ENGLISH
Hananpacha	Sky
Mayu, Yaku	River
Sacha	Forest, Jungle
Yura	Tree

Mom said her parents wanted her to speak Kichwa so she could help them learn the language. "They asked me, 'What is that? What is that?'" When I was a child, I thought it was a smart idea, having your kid learn a language for you.

Now that I have worked in early childhood education and raised a child of my own, I am saddened by my grandparents' choice. Since they were not fluent in their daughter's primary language and spoke to her mainly in a language that was also not their own, they could only name objects or give simple commands. They could not hold a back-and-forth conversation with my mother. (See Figure 5.)

Fig. 5, The value of parent-child communication

Back-and-forth communication with a child allows parents to:

- understand their child as an individual
- learn what their child needs so they can try to provide it
- show through listening that they value their child
- help their child understand and express emotions
- transmit their values, not solely their rules

My grandparents could not sing songs to my mother in Kichwa or speak to her with nuance in either Kichwa or Spanish. They could

[10] The Spanish language appropriated some Kichwa words; a few of those words also migrated into English, including *condor, llama, poncho,* and *puma.*

not tell her stories other than by reading aloud from their Spanish Bible.[11] If Kinti had questions—and what child is not filled with them?—her parents could not give answers beyond the lexicon they memorized.

At the assisted-living center in Seattle, an employee named Juan was a former refugee student of my mother's, and I transcribed several conversations in Spanish between the two of them. One evening, while I fed Mom a cupcake in the garden, she introduced Juan to me (again) and said, *I was helping him learn English and now he can do anything.*

Her belief about Juan learning English echoed the stories my grandmother told about the school she and my grandfather built in the rainforest.

When I was a child, every few years, my grandmother took a Greyhound bus from Minnesota to visit us in California. It was a three-day bus ride, and she smelled of sweat and talcum powder when we hugged her hello. At home, she showered and put on a clean homemade dress, pinned her long white hair in a bun at the nape of her neck, and gathered my sisters and me at her feet to tell us stories about the rainforest. One story was about the Kichwa women who worked for her, the ones she called Rosa and Clotilde.

"They had no tears," my grandmother said, "even if one of their relatives died."

As a child, I accepted my grandmother's words. Now I think to ask: *Did the women never cry, or never when my grandparents could see them?*

Another story was about my grandfather and a Kichwa translator who traveled to all the villages within a three-day canoe ride. My

---

[11] In 1531, Francisco Pizarro brought the first Spanish Bible to what is now called Ecuador. He also brought his belief that colonizing the people and taking their resources was a virtuous act.

grandfather tried to convince the elders to send their boys to his school.

"He said if they learned Spanish, they could get jobs in the city," my grandmother told my sisters and me. "If they learned Spanish, they could do anything."

Mom believed learning English would do the same for Juan.

ANALYSIS OF THEME 2: LANGUAGES AND OTHER PEOPLE'S CHOICES

My mother's ability to speak Spanish remained strong while her Alzheimer's progressed. Since she spoke Spanish before she spoke English, this could be an example of Alzheimer's restoring a felt sense of childhood.

Yet Kichwa is buried within her. As Alzheimer's continues to plunder her memories, is it possible that my mom will begin using her first language, the one she spoke in the jungle?

Theme 3: Missionary school and colonialism

This is a good school, but I will find my way out of it.

QUANTIFICATION

Although my mother said the word *school* sixty-six times in the transcripts, context indicates she referred to the boarding school in only four conversations. For example: *It was our first church—not church but a military type.*

PATIENT HISTORY FOR THEME 3: MISSIONARY SCHOOL AND COLONIALISM

In August 1941, a few weeks after my mother's seventh birthday, her parents waved goodbye to her. As employees of the Christian and Missionary Alliance, they were required to send her to an Alliance boarding school.

A black-and-white photo records my mother's last morning in the jungle. She is outside in a wooden chair, smiling, with a white bandage wrapped around one knee. Moments after her parents took the photo, they strapped her to the chair and handed her off. Three Indigenous men took turns carrying her over the Andes on a multiday journey to Quito.

My mother did not see her parents again until the following summer, at the Alliance's annual retreat. Year after year, she saw her parents for two weeks in the summer. She never returned to the jungle. She never saw Rosa and Clotilde again, or the river, or the path where she had run barefoot since she was two years old. Like Eve, she was cast out of the Garden of Eden.

At the boarding school, no one spoke Kichwa, and Mom lost that language. The teachers called her Janet. No one called her Kinti anymore.

A 2009 United Nations report on Indigenous people, written by Andrea Smith, said Indigenous children in many colonized countries were sent to boarding schools "set up by Christian missions as part of a 'civilization' process." One theme in postcolonial criticism is otherness: Colonialism ruptures Indigenous people from their land, culture, language, and identity.

Not all of the Kichwa people living in the rainforest lost their culture. The Sarayaku people in eastern Ecuador, for example, successfully fought to hold onto their land and villages. But many of the Kichwa boys at my grandparents' school lost their ties to the rainforest when they moved to the cities.

My mother also lost her ties to the rainforest. She was not colonized, though: She was a white child who lived and played in the jungle until she was seven years old.

When children are raised outside their parents' culture, sociologists call them "third culture kids." The land where the children grow up is the closest they know to a home, yet they are expected to return to their parents' homeland, which does not belong to them. My mom was a more-than-three-culture kid. (See Figure 6.)

Our mother rarely talked about the mission school when my sisters and I were young. Once, while she brushed my younger sister's hair, Mom commented that the bristle side of a hairbrush hurts more

Fig. 6, My mother's cultures

- First: her parents' Scandinavian culture, which was withheld from her
- Second: the Ecuadorian rainforest, which she thought of as home
- Third: the mission school
- Fourth: the US, which was her children's homeland yet felt foreign to her
- Is Alzheimer's my mother's fifth culture?

than the flat side when you are being punished. Another time, she said, "I remember hearing children scream at night."

The fragments we heard echoed stories of abuse at the Alliance school in Mamou, Guinea, which was documented by an independent commission of inquiry. In 1998, I read about the Commission's report in a story by David Briggs in *The Seattle Times.* The headline read, "At School In Africa, The Children Of Missionaries Lived In A Secret Hell." I cut out the article, and the next time Mom invited me to dinner at her condo in Seattle, I tried to hand it to her.

"Is this what happened in Quito?" I asked.

She read the headline and pushed my hand away.

I wanted to know more about missionaries in Ecuador. In 1995, Gerard Colby and Charlotte Dennett completed almost two decades of research and published their findings in *Thy Will Be Done: The Conquest of the Amazon: Nelson Rockefeller and Evangelism in the Age of Oil.* (See Figure 7.)

"Did you know your parents were colonizers?" I asked my mom after learning about the oil and missionaries connection. My voice was tight like a dead bolt, the way I often spoke to her before I became a mother and began to see her as a struggling human like me.

I munched on sticks of jicama while my mom rolled enchiladas, and I used the sticks as pointers to list fact after fact about the connections between the oil conglomerates and missionaries. Finally, my mom turned her head away and looked out the window.

Fig. 7, Highly abridged summary of *Thy Will Be Done*, annotated with references to Ecuador

1. Oil companies began prospecting for oil in Ecuador in the 1920s. They wanted to build pipelines through the Amazon.

2. Oil company executives financially supported missionary organizations in South America.

3. Missionaries in South America taught Indigenous people Spanish so they could read the Bible.

4. Some Indigenous people moved to the cities, where they could get jobs because they spoke Spanish.

5. Oil companies discovered major oil reserves in Ecuador in the late 1960s.

6. With fewer Indigenous people living in the Amazon rainforest, it was easier for oil companies to build pipelines. Ecuador began exporting oil in 1972.

After a few moments, she asked, "I wonder if that's why one of the missions was called Shell?"[12] Half an hour later, while she pulled enchiladas out of the oven, she said, "I wonder if that's why our church needed to help refugees with the Sanctuary Movement?"

Later, though, while she scooped seeds out of a papaya for our dessert, Mom said, "My parents, the Alliance, they couldn't have known."

Almost half a century later, she would not question the ethics of the missionary organization. She would not doubt her parents, who believed so fervently in their mission they were willing to forsake their own child. I wonder if my mother had to absolve the Alliance and her parents so the sacrifice made of her childhood would feel worth it.

[12] Yes, it was. In the 1930s, Shell Oil Company built an airstrip and small town in central Ecuador. A decade later, missionary pilots began using the airstrip and established a mission there.

ANALYSIS OF THEME 3: MISSIONARY SCHOOL AND COLONIALISM

Desmond Tutu said, "When the missionaries came to Africa, they had the Bible, and we had the land. They said, 'Let us pray.' We closed our eyes. When we opened them, we had the Bible, and they had the land."

My mother grew up in what felt to her like an enchanted forest because her parents wanted to teach Indigenous boys a European language to overpower the one they already spoke. For Mom, the jungle was play and pretending; for Indigenous culture, it was predators and prey. My mother was torn from the jungle, but so were other children.

As the child of colonizers, indoctrinated in their beliefs, if my mom had stayed in Ecuador, would she have acted out her parents' conviction that severing people from their culture was a righteous act?

That is a hypothetical. The reality is that my mother lost the language and culture of her beloved jungle, and she was delivered to a mission system that allowed, according to the Alliance Commission's report, an "atmosphere of great terror."

Theme 4: Depression and delight

Opening a gift bag and finding socks: *Oh, my goodness! You don't know how good that is because everything I've done, I've done with feet.*

QUANTIFICATION

My mother's vocabulary became notably positive after she was diagnosed with Alzheimer's. Common words included *good* (333 instances), *love* (138), *happy* (73), and *amazing* (26).

For comparison, she described something as *bad* or *feeling badly* only fourteen times.

PATIENT HISTORY FOR THEME 4: DEPRESSION AND DELIGHT

Some Alzheimer's patients grow negative, belligerent, and aggressive, while others are described by family members as becoming their sweetest self. My mom is in the latter group. After examining my mother in the memory care unit, her physician wrote, "Patient asked me if I could sing and dance with her." He added a smiley-face emoji to the medical notes.

Our mother's joyful nature while under the influence of Alzheimer's contrasts with the depression she experienced when my sisters and I were young.

Before she developed Alzheimer's, Mom showed strong feelings of guilt over the smallest errors.

"Once the dementia kicked in, she forgot she was supposed to be a good enough Christian," Thora said.

Apprehension about doing something she believed was wrong, which our pre-dementia mother would have labeled sinful, disappeared when she slid into Alzheimer's: *I'm not one bit worried about yes or no or yes or no.*

"Would you say she was trying to hide her mistakes or that she made excuses or that she blamed other people?" I asked in a sister Zoom. The consensus was all three.

"With Alzheimer's, she has the freedom to be herself. No shame, no guilt," added Greta.

"I like Mom more now," said Sigrid.

So do I.

We remember our mother's depression starting when our youngest sister was a toddler, when I was seven or eight years old.

"That's when you started taking care of me," Greta told me over Zoom. I usually watched my sisters' faces on the screen, but I looked up at the laptop camera so my baby sister would know I heard her.

We remember Mom's depression lifted when Greta was a high school senior, the year before our mother left our father. Before that, though, "She was always in bed," Greta said. My baby sister corrected herself: Our mom went to work and church, and took care of household tasks, but she "took to bed when she could. She didn't want to have to make decisions."

We dissected her depression. "She never felt worthy enough," said Thora. "It's tied to sin. She thought she was an unworthy mother and wife."

Musing together led us to the missionary boarding school our mother attended, which proclaimed through words and acts that children were sinful and needed to be controlled. Women and girls, especially, must be on high alert to keep themselves from transgressing. Mom learned the message as though it were nailed to the schoolhouse door. (See Figure 8.)

Fig. 8, What the mission school taught our mom about sin, presented as a resolution

> WHEREAS, in the Garden of Eden, Eve was curious and decided to eat the fruit of knowledge even though it was not allowed, committing the original sin; and
>
> WHEREAS, Eve then tempted Adam to sin by telling him to eat the fruit of knowledge, and, helpless, he did; and
>
> WHEREAS, Eve was a woman and Adam a man;
>
> NOW THEREFORE BE IT RESOLVED by 1 Timothy 2:11-14, "I do not permit a woman to teach or to exercise authority over a man; rather, she is to remain quiet . . . For Adam was not deceived, but the woman was deceived and became a transgressor."

"Depression and oppressive 'morality' were two sides of the same coin," Sigrid said.

On one of our Zoom nights in February, Sigrid was busy at the hospital and could not join us. Thora, Greta, and I, however, poured glasses of wine in our separate cities and turned on our screens. At one point, I recalled that our mother tried to leave our father when Greta was a toddler. Had our mother decided to build her own garden?

When she told the church pastor, though, he told her it would be a sin. "Mom told me he quoted the apostle Paul," I said, "that wives have to obey their husbands."[13]

"Wait, when was that?" asked Greta.

"When we lived in Bakersfield," said Thora, and I thought, *how do people piece their childhoods together when they do not have a band of sisters?*

Years later, a different pastor told our mom she had the right to make her own decision about divorce. When Greta left for college, our mother left, too.

"Can you imagine the guts it took for her to leave Dad and go back to teaching?" asked Thora.

Greta remembered that after the divorce, Mom told her, "I shouldn't feel guilty about doing what I need to do."

"But she did feel guilty," I said, and my sisters nodded their heads in their little Zoom boxes.

At the next week's Zoom, we shared our ideas with Sigrid, who asked, "If she'd had somebody to talk to, to say, 'You don't have to feel guilty,' can you imagine what Mom would have been like?"

ANALYSIS OF THEME 4: DEPRESSION AND DELIGHT

Our mother's current happiness contrasts with the lengthy depression she experienced pre-Alzheimer's. My sisters remember that in stories about the jungle, our mom sounded "free," "self-confident," and "worthy." That confidence shriveled in the mission school climate where children could never be good enough. Could Alzheimer's be a gale strong enough to extinguish her decades of shame?

I wonder if it is common for dementia to cleave people from their long-held moral beliefs. A study about ethical transformation in Alzheimer's patients would be beneficial.

---

[13] This belief is shared by 69 percent of Christian nationalists in the US, according to the 2023 PRRI/Brookings Institute poll, "A Christian Nation? Understanding the Threat of Christian Nationalism to American Democracy and Culture."

DISCUSSION

Three themes in postcolonial criticism helped me untangle my jungle of notes.

INTERNALIZED COLONIALISM

Mental health professionals use the Colonial Mentality Scale to research the well-being of people whose cultures were colonized. When Indigenous people internalize the colonizers' negative messages, depression tends to increase. In particular, Indigenous children who are forcibly removed from their cultures may grow up to believe they do not have the power to make choices for themselves.

I see a parallel to this research in my mother's experience. She was not colonized, yet the missionary-colonizer mentality of her parents and teachers—and their message that because Mom was a "transgressor" she must submit to male authority—may have led to her long-term depression.

Not all Indigenous people internalize the messages of the colonizers. Half a century after my mother left the rainforest, Noemí Gualinga of the Sarayaku community grew up to be a Kichwa rights activist. When the government of Ecuador allowed an oil company to drill in Sarayaku territory, Noemi was one of the community leaders who petitioned the Inter-American Court of Human Rights. After a decade of legal battle, the court ruled the Sarayaku people have the "right of consent" over oil projects on their ancestral land.

Noemi's daughters, Nina and Helena Gualinga, watched their mother's activism and internalized her sense of power. "It was always a part of my life that people were fighting for our communities," the younger daughter said in *Helena Sarayaku Manta* ("Helena of the Sarayaku People"), a documentary about her environmental activism.

LOSS OF MEMORY

By raising their children on ancestral land, the Sarayaku people held onto their memories. In an April 2022 interview in *Vogue,* Nina Gualinga said, "When I wear Wituk paint, when I sing the songs of my grandmother and great-grandmother, when I speak the Kichwa language with my son, I feel the presence of all those, all my ancestors, who transmitted this to me."

When colonialism succeeds in destroying a culture, however, Indigenous people struggle to know: How did my ancestors live on the land? What did they believe? What would they have named me? Colonialism steals the memories of a people.

In a distant echo, Alzheimer's steals the memories of a person.

The first time my mother did not recognize me—when she stood pale and naked in the assisted-living studio—it felt as though I were orphaned. Alzheimer's loops up and down, however, and for a year, she would sometimes know me, sometimes not. Now, I don't expect my mom to see me as her daughter. Now, I am glad she is freed from the memories which for so long strapped her down.

RESISTANCE

Postcolonial criticism examines how some people resist the colonizing beliefs and reclaim their identity.

Although my mom physically escaped the mission school in 1951, the shame she was taught grew into a decades-long depression. She left my father and returned to teaching, which were acts of resistance, yet she continued to fill her journal with prayers to overcome her sinful nature. What if embracing Alzheimer's was another form of resistance?

Five hundred years ago, the Catholic church created a Doctrine of Discovery, which encouraged men like Francisco Pizarro to subjugate non-Europeans, convert them to Christianity, and confiscate their land. On March 30, 2023, after decades of protests by Indigenous people around the world, the Vatican finally rescinded this doctrine.

On August 20, 2023, the Ecuadorian people passed a referendum to ban all oil drilling in the vast Yasuní National Park. Yasuní, just northeast of the Sarayaku territory, might be the most biodiverse land on the planet. In a CNN interview, Helena Gualinga said, "This referendum presents a huge opportunity for us to create change in a tangible way."[14]

CONCLUSION

When I was young, I was in love with my mom. In photos, my hands wrapped around her arm or my body leaned against hers. She was my Garden of Eden, where I felt safe and treasured.

Her depression started when I was at the end of my Preoperational Stage. When Mom burrowed into her bed, it uprooted the garden she'd built for me. By middle school, I resented her: Why wasn't she interested in me? Here is another way to think about it: Because my mom loved me so well in my early years, I knew what love was supposed to feel like and judged her for tearing it away.

As an adult, I would hug her quickly, then push her away. My mother was unhappy, so I turned from her and sought my own happiness. I would build my own garden.

I cast her aside like my grandparents had done to her, and that is how we lived for many years. I tried to be polite to her. I bought her scarves.

In this thematic analysis, while exploring my research question—can Alzheimer's restore the felt sense of a person's early childhood?—a kindred question emerged. Did my mother's Alzheimer's do the same for me? Did it carry me back to my Preoperational Stage?

Alzheimer's came, and my mom reawakened. When I visited the assisted-living center, I rubbed her back and smoothed her hair. I held her hand while we chatted, and it felt like I was seven.

One day, while we walked through the garden, she said, *As long as there's birds up there, I'm okay,* and I felt grateful for the disease that brought her back to my sisters and me. I would say it as a prayer if I still followed her religion: "Thank you, thank you," I would whisper while holding my mother's hand.

---

[14] In 2023, Helena Gualinga spoke about Indigenous people's leadership in the fight against climate change at both the United Nations Climate Change Conference in New York City and the World Economic Forum in Davos.

CHECKLIST FOR A SIGN-MAKING PARTY

"Can I have people over to make signs on Saturday?" Indigo called from the staircase. It was January 2017, and the Women's March in Seattle would be one of thousands taking place around the world.

"Of course," I said before putting down my laptop and rising from the daybed. "Does that mean you're going without me and Dad?"

"You can come," they said. That day, Indigo's head was shaved on one side and long, wavy hair on the other, colored its natural brown. My high schooler turned away, willing to march but not chitchat with me.

"How many friends will be here?" I called to the back of their head.

"Like, four."

I never knew, in those teenage years, if Indigo would laugh and hug me or scowl and shut the door. When they were younger, they enjoyed my extroversion. Big, blonde, loud, and happy, now I was too much. I tried to love them from the background, spreading Nutella on graham crackers for an afternoon snack, like when they were four years old, safe upstairs in their bedroom, wearing fuzzy footsie pajamas.

Sometimes, I fumbled.

One time in the TSA line at the airport, while we shuffled toward the scanner, Indigo leaned into me and whispered, "You don't know what it's like, Mom, people staring at your body."

"You think I don't know?" I asked, which was decades of true but not the truth my baby needed. I saw it in their eyes, the fear that I would never understand, and quickly said, "It must be so hard. I'm sorry." I reached to rub their shoulder, but they shrugged me away.

After Indigo went upstairs, I watched the empty staircase and wondered if I could find a way to help my child. They knew we had art supplies since I ran a preschool. But why confine the teenagers to little children's leftovers? I could give them a sign-making party.

I heard Indigo close their bedroom door and returned to my laptop. My little dog, Pugsley, now lay where I had made the daybed warm. A squirrel distracted me by bounding along the fig tree outside our living room window. My mind bounced from the newsletter I needed to write, to phone calls I owed, to breakfast dishes still in the sink. I would need to get supplies for the sign-making party. I would need to clean the house.

I know how to do this, I thought. I would welcome the teens, yet not take over their party. I would be as imperceptible as furniture so Indigo would not mind my being in the room. I opened a new document and typed "Activity Checklist" at the top.

☑ PREP THE WORKSPACE

Before the sign-making party, I covered my dining room table with a plastic shower curtain because children are known to leave pen marks. An hour later, seven teenagers sat at the table, sharing chairs and coloring signs. Seven teens, five genders, four ethnicities. Indigo's friend Sammi teensplained the difference between pansexual and bisexual to me, and while she talked, she pressed her marker into the shower curtain and left an ink spot two inches around.

Earlier that morning, while the kids disappeared into our dining room, two Eastside couples huddled at our front door.

Tai's mom asked, "Will you and Jason stay with them the whole time?"

"They'll stick to each other," I said, "and Jason and I will stick with them."

"What if someone gets separated?" asked the other mom.

Until our child started high school, we had lived east of the city. In the suburbs, children grow up in fenced backyards and well-groomed parks with their parents' eyes scanning like drones overhead. Indigo had never crossed a street on their own until we moved to the city. Half of Indigo's friends, many of whom were also queer, still lived in those suburbs and needed their parents to drive them to Seattle across the Lake Washington Bridge.

"Your kids have cell phones," I told the parents. "I'll make sure they have Jason's and my numbers before we leave for the march."

Tai's mom leaned against her husband and struggled with her boots while the other couple left, then she bent toward me and whispered, "He's not a city kid like Indigo."

"But you want him to be," I whispered back.

At the preschool where I taught, I asked parents to let their children walk through the classroom door all by themselves. "Your children want to be independent," I told them. It's Child Development 101.

In my front entry now, either the mom's zipper was stuck on her boot or she was pretending.

"It's like a field trip," I told her. "I suppose I could have brought home the preschoolers' walking rope."

She laughed. Her boot zipped up. The couple left.

After that first sign-making party, our house became the meeting place for several years of marches. Until the teens started driving themselves to our home, I set up the worktable where it was visible from the front door. When nervous parents from the suburbs walked their teens up to our house, they saw happy children coloring with markers.

For straight parents who think their child might be queer, love is mixed with fear and inexperience. In our teenage years, decades ago, boys were supposed to keep their hair short, girls were supposed to keep their legs together, and queer people were supposed to keep hidden until they moved to the big city. The other parents and I were not raised with a checklist for when our children come out as transgender, nonbinary, or pansexual.

I love throwing parties, so that's what I did. When Indigo came out as transgender, Jason and I put invitations in our neighbors' mailboxes for a cookie celebration after work on Friday night. I have since been accused of being rah-rah about my child being trans, but making myself the center of people's attention is my version of fight-or-flight. Indigo came out almost a decade ago, when movies showed transgender people as prostitutes or psychopaths. Parents with trans children posted online that they lost all their friends. One family had to move after someone killed their dog.

I wanted the people who surrounded our child to be different. "Celebrate with us," I told everyone we knew.

Our neighbors joined us that Friday night for cookies. The conservative family who lived next door even brought a gift. "I wasn't sure what you do for this," the mother whispered to me.

Some of the parents of Indigo's rainbow-loving group of friends jumped into the uncertainty. One morning, while sipping our lattes, another mom and I walked along a muddy path in a Seattle park. My friend told me she and her husband believed their son was gay. They wanted to be the good kind of parents, she said, and the night before, they had knocked on their son's bedroom door and sat together on his bed.

"We want you to know we will always love you," the dad said. "You can tell us if you're gay."

"I'm not gay," their child said.

"We know you might be scared to tell us."

"I'm not gay."

"Would you feel safe to tell us if you were?"

"Yes. But I'm not gay."

The mom asked if I could check with Indigo, and Indigo said, "Yeah, he's straight."

☑ DECORATE THE HOUSE

I put every kind of rainbow flag I could find in the flowerpot on the front porch. I hung shiny bead necklaces on the coat hooks for anyone who needed to sparkle. It's like taping family photos to the preschoolers' cubbies or letting three-year-olds hold stuffed animals during circle time. I wanted the children to feel safe.

That's not the only reason I decorated. One year during Pride, which in Seattle lasts the whole month of June, Jason and I walked past a giant Craftsman house a few blocks from our home. The show-off house had flags and rainbow bunting strung along its balconies.

"I want bunting," I told Jason.

Fabric bunting is expensive, but I found rainbow tablecloths at the dollar store, taped them together, and made my own. And I had more flags.

"Did you win Pride this year?" asked Jason.

Maybe the parents who saw my rainbow bunting thought I knew how to support my transgender nonbinary teen. But if you're a hammer, you hit a nail; if you're exuberant, you throw a party. I wanted to have the most rainbow-covered house and throw the best sign-making parties. Maybe I believed if I did those things, my child would know how much I loved them. Maybe I believed if I won Pride, it would keep my baby safe.

One boy kept clothing at our house. After his parents dropped him off at the sign-making parties, he ran upstairs to change into something floral. His mom knew about the clothes and sometimes squeezed my hand when she and her husband said goodbye.

One kid said their parents never mentioned queer people. Those parents, however, had said supportive things to me when Indigo came out as trans in middle school, and they drove their teen to our house on the morning of the Pride parade. Teenagers see their parents as fully grown, as unable to still be growing.

I remember the Saturday our family walked a few miles through Seattle to eat lunch at Americana. Casey, one of the high school art teachers, was on the weekend waitstaff and stopped by our table. Holding a tray above her shoulder, she told Jason and me about an independent project Indigo was working on.

"They're using variations in color to explore negative space," Casey said. I didn't completely understand but sensed it meant something good.

Indigo grinned while the art teacher walked away, and I leaned over to kiss their half-shaved head.

"You should feel proud," I nodded.

"It's not that, Mom," my teenager said. "She called me 'they.'"

Indigo had told me that when they were misgendered, it felt like a slap, but I didn't understand until I saw them smiling. I was still growing. I am still growing.

☑ PLAY MUSIC

The teenagers seemed to know all the words to the songs they played in our home. I didn't know many lyrics to popular music when I was a child. My mother grew up in a mission school and was introduced to Broadway musicals when she moved to the United States: I was raised on hymns and show tunes.

When my sister, Thora, was six, and I was four, our mother taught us the words to "I Whistle a Happy Tune" from *The King and I*. Our two younger sisters were a toddler and a newborn, and Mom couldn't pack us all up to take Thora to school, so my sister had to walk several blocks and cross a major intersection alone. If she felt scared, our mother said, she should stand up straight and whistle that happy tune.

"You're a big girl," Mom told her, so I stood at the front door and watched my sister march off to first grade, armed with a song. Before I started kindergarten, I learned to whistle the fear away. Act happy. Keep walking. When Indigo transitioned, I made myself the center of attention. I knew how to project the sweetness of my preschool teacher voice. Look at me, the mother of a transgender child. Keep your focus on me and leave my baby alone. I wasn't trying to be rah-rah. I was afraid of what people would do to my child, so I wrapped myself around Indigo as though both of us were trans. Whistling while I walked.

At Indigo's eighth-grade graduation, the twenty-minute slideshow highlighted every student except one. Four of my child's classmates had been put in charge of choosing the photos. Mina, the only girl in the group, told her mother the boys wanted to make fun of Indigo by selecting photos that looked like the gender my child had been assigned at birth. Mina's mother called me, and I called the supervising adult.

"We want the students to own the process," said the volunteer. "If you don't like the photos they are choosing, we can take out all of the pictures of Indigo."

"Could Mina choose the photos?" I suggested.

"Oh, no. We value student collaboration."

I stopped arguing for the photos. Jason and I had already fought for Indigo to not be segregated on the overnight trip and for our child's name to be updated in the yearbook. Indigo said the slideshow didn't matter; what mattered was that Mina tried to help.

I worried there wouldn't be enough Minas in high school, and my fear was hard to whistle away, yet Indigo kept walking. Within a year, they no longer needed me to shelter them with my loudness, and I no longer knew how to help.

But Indigo gathered a fine group of friends who connected their phones to our speakers and chose the music for the sign-making parties—although they never played any of their songs all the way through.

☑ BUY POSTER MARKERS

Giant Sharpies can last through three years' worth of marches if the caps are closed securely. Preschoolers are good at replacing the caps, but teenagers have other priorities. A high schooler might forget to close a marker because they're interested in the kid sitting across the table. (The teens at our sign-making parties dated each other like loop-de-loop.) Or a teen might be a little pisser and deliberately not close his markers, although that might be the most rebellious thing he did all day.

I tried to not give reminders to put on the caps. The kids were going to a march where a bad someone might call out a gender slur or racist word, or a good someone might accidentally use the wrong pronoun. It takes energy to be different, and I didn't want the teenagers spending their energy snapping the caps.

When they came out in middle school, Indigo was in the spotlight. Tired of being the Transgender Kid, weary of the stares and comments, they applied to an arts high school in Seattle. When they got in, we moved.

It wasn't only for the high school. We wanted to live in the city.

It wasn't only for the city.

In our old neighborhood, the kids grew up free to roam between homes, and a few weeks after the cookie celebration, a child from the end of the neighborhood ran in circles around Indigo in our yard, calling my middle schooler's old name over and over. I heard the yelling, went outside, and sent the child home. After calling his parents, who apologized, I told my baby it wouldn't happen again.

The next day, the child stood in the yard next door and called out the old name. Again, I called his family. The other neighbors rallied: The child was old enough to know he was hurting Indigo. The neighbors said he couldn't use their yards.

He stood on the street and screamed my child's old name. I called his parents. I begged them. Indigo refused to go outside or to invite friends over.

We wanted to move to the city anyway.

☑ BUY FOAM BOARD FOR THE SIGNS

Preschoolers write their names with gigantic first initials, shrinking each letter as they go and often running out of space at the end of the line. Teenagers' first attempts at sign-writing look the same.

"I ran out of room," Sammi groaned, and I knew she was thinking, as every teen does, that everyone would notice.

I wanted to whisper, "Oh, sweet child, if someone sees your funny letters, it will make them love you even more." But it was not my place to say that, not in a room full of high schoolers. Besides, those words would not be true. Being different would not always make those teenagers beloved.

We were lucky to live in Seattle, where some of the crosswalks are painted with rainbows. My child could walk around the city with neon or half-shaved hair and rarely be harassed.

The rhyme about sticks and stones makes harassment sound benign until one has held their breath, waiting for it to end. One summer, while Indigo was in high school—the summer their hair was fluorescent green—we spent a week in Rome. At airport security, our family walked past a row of *polizia*, each man boasting an automatic rifle like a sash across his chest. One of the men muttered the slur for gay that starts with "F," and I looked at him, mama-bear angry. Keeping eye contact with me, he flicked his chin toward my child and rubbed his hand up and down the barrel of his gun.

☑ SET UP A GLITTER STATION

At the preschool, I often had glitter-butt by the end of the day. It was worth it: Children love the shiny magic that is sprinkled from a jar. I tried to get the high schoolers to do their glitter-sprinkling over the kitchen sink to make my cleanup easier, but it didn't matter since the kids would shake their festive signs while walking through my home. Our big dog Toby's long white fur needed multiple brushings to get the sparkles out, and no matter how much I vacuumed, magical fairy dust twinkled for months in the cracks of our floorboards. I wanted to reserve glitter for Pride events, but the first time I didn't put it out, Tai asked, "Where's the glitter?"

Jason and I went with them to the Seattle Pride Parade until the summer when Indigo's hair was dyed fluorescent green. The high schoolers, looking glorious in their wild or subtle rainbow gear—depending on the outness of the child—said they wanted me to drop them off across from the Space Needle.

"You don't want to see the whole parade?" I asked.

"We've seen it," one of them said, and I realized the excitement was in the shadow of the Space Needle where they would meet their friends. I remembered being their age and hoping I would see a boy I liked. I remembered believing my life could change with one encounter.

For the Trans Pride parade that year, also in June, it was just our little family. Indigo had long ago stopped holding Jason's and my hands and begging us to count to three and fly them up with a giant swing. Still, we walked together, with Indigo between us. Most people know someone who is lesbian or gay. Someone being trans is less familiar: The unfamiliar stimulates adrenaline, which goads the impulse to fight. Jason and I walked, like flag-waving bodyguards, on either side of Indigo.

The parade started near Seattle Central College. We tried to ignore the fanatic with the giant black sign, who screamed that our child was going to hell, but I watched a gender-nonconforming individual walk up and kiss the screamer on the cheek. It made the screaming almost festive. It made me wish that I, too, could kiss the danger away.

☑ THINK OF SAYINGS FOR THE SIGNS

Indigo attended their first march in a stroller. At the base of the Space Needle, while two thousand people chanted for an end to gun violence, our toddler napped with their head hanging over the side of the stroller. After that, it was Pride parades, kid-friendly marches, and candlelight vigils in city parks. Jason and I talked about why we attended. Was it to teach Indigo what we believed? Look-at-me righteousness? The excitement of loud, stomping crowds?

Now, it was the teenagers' turn. Over the years, the teens in my house made signs for immigrants' rights, Black Lives Matter, love is love.

But at the first sign-making party, they stared at blank rectangles before pulling out their phones to gather ideas. Another time, a high schooler in a fedora brought a list of fifty sayings he had collected online from marches outside of Seattle. *When that kid grows up,* I thought, *he will host the sign-making parties.*

Eventually, they came up with their own messages—some of which made me laugh, some of which were inappropriate. "Damn right we're snowflakes . . . and winter is coming," said a sign for the Women's March. "Grab 'em by the patriarchy," said another. For the March for Science, one of the kids wrote, "Science is the cure for bullshit."

When I wasn't replenishing supplies, I hid in the kitchen with Jason. We listened to their conversations—how they pretended they knew things they didn't, yet how they knew so much more than I did at their age. They used words like *resonant* and *intersectional,* and Jason and I sometimes had to look up definitions with our two heads huddled over his phone.

☑ ASK JASON TO MAKE HIS CHOCOLATE CHIP COOKIES

At the first sign-making party, my husband baked the cookies while the kids were coloring signs. When the scent of brown sugar and melted chocolate reached the dining room, the teens looked up, expectant. I hoped the fragrance murmured love. No matter how many cookies Jason made before the marches, the plate was empty when the kids huddled at our front door to put on their shoes.

At one of the marches, we saw a bear of a dog, a Newfoundland, standing on the sidewalk. Its muzzle was grey and white. A man held the dog's leash and cheered the people walking past.

"Does your dog want to march with us?" asked one of the teens, and we stopped so the kids could pet the bear.

"He can't walk that far," said the man. "I could march, or I could bring my dog, and I figured it would help people more if I brought my dog."

He shared his Newfoundland, Jason made homemade cookies, and I threw those sign-making parties for the teens. I hoped our small offerings would protect them.

☑ LEAVE FOR THE MARCH

After the first sign-making party, the kids jumped around the porch and played swordfight with their signs. I made them line up for a photo while Jason locked the door.

Many parties later, when most of the kids no longer needed their parents to drive them to our house, Indigo left the sign-coloring in the dining room and joined me in the kitchen.

"We want to go to the march on our own," they said and leaned their head on my shoulder.

"Of course, baby," I said. I wanted that, too. Child Development 101.

The teenagers' lives—even in my home, using my materials—faced away from me. They were supposed to face away. I was supposed to watch from behind. Still, when they were ready to go, I felt Eastside-parent nervous and asked them to let me take a photo. They posed with their arms around each other, children in sight of adulthood.

My child would go to marches on their own, to college on their own, into the world without me. I would not be there to gather attention away from Indigo. We swing our children by their hands, and then we set them free and watch them fly away from us. I didn't know how to make the world safe for my child, so I put out the glitter. I bought enough foam board. I smiled and tried to stay quiet.

ACKNOWLEDGMENTS

When I lived in San Francisco after college, I scribbled poems and short stories in cafés and wondered if I could ever be a writer. I was lucky to find a different profession that I loved just as much when I became a teacher, and my writing veered to newsletters and emails to parents. Decades later, the pandemic hit, and I gave myself permission to listen to the voice inside me that whispered my answer to, "If you could do anything, what would it be?"

I signed up for a beginning memoir class with Theo Nestor at Hugo House in Seattle and began learning the craft of creative nonfiction writing. Our classes were online, due to the pandemic, yet Theo created such a warm environment that many of us continue to write together years later. Thank you, Theo, for encouraging your students to submit our work to literary journals.

I am grateful to Sonora Jha for her introduction to essays class at Hugo House, also online. One day, I had a breakthrough—oh, you don't just say a shirt is blue, you choose details that help tell the story!—and Sonora laughed in her Zoom box and let me know she saw my click of understanding.

I took another Hugo House essay class with Beth Slattery, who created such a lovely workshop that a group of us asked to keep working with her, and we still do. Beth also provided essential line-by-line critique for almost all of the essays in *Bigger*.

I workshopped the essays in this book with my two writing groups, who pointed out gaps and encouraged me to dig deeper, especially emotionally. I am grateful to each of you, and you will see insights you shared with me woven through this book. Lacey Leavitt Gray, Uma Kukathas, Vani Mandava, and Beth Slattery: I look forward to more writing train trips to Portland and writing retreats at the beach. Su Cummings, Stacey Jones, and Darryl Price: From our first in-person meeting at a picnic table in Volunteer Park to making the rounds of our Seattle homes, we have grown together as writers. Stacey and Uma, I value our dedicated writing times at Hugo House, cafés, and the library.

I began sending my essay collection to independent presses in the fall of 2023 and, to take my mind off it, attended a winter residency through Pacific University on the snowy beach in Seaside, Oregon. The fiction, nonfiction, and poetry craft talks were so brilliant, as well as Pacific MFA Director Scott Korb's leadership, that I enrolled in the low-residency program. Thank you to fellow students Rebecca Weller, Rachel Lincoln Sarnoff, and Amy Roost for making sure we balanced study with celebration.

I was fortunate to develop another writing group through the MFA program and value my monthly discussions about writing and literature—online, since we span the country—with Gina Calderone, Susan Hata, and Lauren Daley-Maurer.

I am grateful to my first advisor, Mike Magnuson, for his "boot camp" that focused on strengthening my sentences and storytelling. Based on extraordinary workshopping with W. Ralph Eubanks (especially comments from my classmates Owólabi Aboyade and Zia Dione), I asked Ralph to be my advisor. He helped me focus on the importance of place (geography, history, culture) and asked probing questions about ideas I hinted at in my writing.

To the Atticus Hotel in McMinnville, Oregon: Thank you for creating an Artist in Residency program and providing a beautiful and welcoming space to write.

Thank you to the authors, contest judges, editors, and volunteer readers at literary journals who were generous with their support. Martha Highers, editor at *Under the Sun,* wrote an encouraging rejection letter (including helpful reader comments) for one of the first essays I ever submitted. Author Emily Bernard judged the Eunice Williams Nonfiction Prize at *HerStry* and wrote a detailed and affirming comment about my essay. Author Sue William Silverman, Creative Nonfiction Editor at *Hunger Mountain,* wrote a rejection letter so positive I felt better than if she'd offered to publish my essay.

Thank you to the editors at the journals that published earlier versions of essays in this book: *Under the Sun,* "Naming My Father"; *North American Review,* "I Am the Dippy Bird"; *HerStry,* "Let Us Sit on the Lawn" (published as "Different From Other Mothers"); *Hippocampus Magazine,* "Checklist for a Sign-Making Party"; *New England Review,* "Resurrecting My Mother's Childhood: A Thematic Analysis."

It has been a joy to work with the editorial team at Autumn House Press. Editor in chief Christine Stroud answered every question and oversaw the process of bringing my book to publication with kindness and deep expertise. I was thrilled to work with my editor, Hattie Fletcher, whose attention to detail and insights about structure and theme helped me revise the essays to make a more cohesive whole. Thank you to author Clifford Thompson, who selected my manuscript for Autumn House's nonfiction prize and wrote such kind words about *Bigger*. The book cover, designed by Joel W. Coggins, is more beautiful than I could have imagined.

Thank you to my friend, photographer Deema Almunajem, for your beautiful work and conversation about creating art.

When my child started school, I dreamed of opening a preschool where children would be valued with all their differences. Thank you to the Pumpkin Team—Kasia Fryczka, Erica Goodman, Annette Miller, and Jerry Soules—for working with me for a dozen years, nurturing our curious and creative kids, and being the best teaching team ever.

When my child came out as transgender, Aidan Key and Kristin Wilson-Key of Gender Diversity surrounded our family with love, support, and information. Thank you! Thank you! You helped us help our child thrive. I encourage families with trans and gender diverse children to visit www.genderdiversity.org.

Thank you to my students and their parents, and to the gender diverse people in my life who teach and inspire me. In my essays, I used pseudonyms and changed some identifying details to protect the safety of people who are gender diverse and the privacy of my former students.

My life has been blessed with friends who are like family, and I am so grateful for their love and support. To Angela Kennedy: We've been there for so many highlights of each other's lives but mostly just to grab a latte and talk about our kids. To Angelene Price and Deina King: Who would have known, when you signed your children up for my brand-new preschool, that we would become the kind of friends who ask the deepest questions of each other? To Beth Syltebo and Bhavya Srivastava, who were there for me in the dark, dark time when the world shut down and my mother forgot I was her daughter: Someday we'll visit London together!

To Carla Bauman and Lucas Schenck, and your beach house and dogs and fresh oysters and lounging by the fire: Here's to many more great meals together! To Kerry Ladd: From team-teaching fourth- and fifth-graders thirty years ago to meeting for our weekly river walks during the pandemic, you have always challenged me to be my best self. To Leisa and René Redelsperger, whom Jason and I so admired as parents that we asked you to be our child's legal guardian if something happened to us (and Leisa clapped her hands and said, "That would be great!"): You are our chosen family.

To Lise Kaye and Liz Bohlin, and the way we celebrate each other's new endeavors. To Mavis Zhang, who sent me sweet videos of her girls when the preschool went on lockdown, brought lightness to that time, and became my walking friend. To Sybil Becker and Jennifer Volckmann McDevitt ("Freak"): You welcomed me into your home when I was in college and couldn't afford my own place, and soon I became Sybil's "daughter" and Jenny's "twin." Thank you for taking in a stranger and making me family. To Theresa Garcia and Lisa Quisito, who love Jason and Indigo and are part of our family: Here's to spending every Valentine's Day and Labor Day together for the rest of our lives. Vivian Yuen and Francis Lau, what a lovely thing for us to become friends while watching each other's children grow to adulthood.

To Diane: I haven't heard your voice in ten years, except in the final voicemail you left. Every few days, when I hear someone cackle or see a giant smile that reminds me of you, I remember again how lucky I am that we both loved to boogie board. You were my biggest supporter while I forged my way from teenager to adult, and I don't know who I would have become without you as my best friend.

To Mom: Our last few years together brought me such joy while I watched your childlike wonder about the world. We laughed and held hands, and I felt the closeness again that I remembered from childhood. The core of who I am came from the love you gave me, and I promise to look up and hear the moon with you.

I am grateful for the love of my in-laws, Bill and Marie Fuller, who told me when I joined their family, "We always said the girl who marries Jason will be the luckiest girl in the world," and they were right.

I am blessed to enjoy invigorating and laugh-filled conversations with my brothers-in-law Aaron and Stephen.

How lucky I am to reconnect with my sisters as adults. When the pandemic and Mom's Alzheimer's could have buried us with grief, instead we turned toward each other in our Sunday-night Zooms, discovered the boxes we had put each other in did not fit, and became friends as well as siblings. Your enthusiastic support for my writing, your willingness to answer my unending questions about our childhood, and your pride in my work, which matches my pride in each of yours, mean everything to me.

Indigo, my darling love, being your mother is my greatest joy.

Jason, you're my favorite. Always.

WINNERS OF THE AUTUMN HOUSE PRESS NONFICTION PRIZE

Deep & Wild: On Mountains, Opossums & Finding Your Way in West Virginia by Laura Jackson, selected by Jenny Boully

Otherwise: Essays by Julie Marie Wade, selected by Lia Purpura

The Running Body by Emily Pifer, selected by Steve Almond

All Who Belong May Enter by Nicholas Ward, selected by Jaquira Díaz

Skull Cathedral: A Vestigial Anatomy by Melissa Wiley, selected by Paul Lisicky

Limited by Body Habitus: An American Fat Story by Jennifer Renee Blevins, selected by Daisy Hernández

Paper Sons: A Memoir by Dickson Lam, selected by Alison Hawthorne Deming

RUN SCREAM UNBURY SAVE by Katherine McCord, selected Michael Martone

Presentimiento: A Life in Dreams by Harrison Candelaria Fletcher, selected by Dinty W. Moore

So Many Africas: Six Years in a Zambian Village by Jill Kandel, selected by Dinty W. Moore

A Greater Monster by Adam Patric Miller, selected by Phillip Lopate

Love for Sale and Other Essays by Clifford Thompson, selected by Phillip Lopate

NEW AND FORTHCOMING FROM AUTUMN HOUSE PRESS

Interlocutor Goddess by Jasmine Reid, winner of the 2024 CAAPP Book Prize, selected by Aracelis Girmay

self-driving by Betsy Fagin, winner of the 2024 Poetry Prize, selected by Kazim Ali

The Great Grown-Up Game of Make-Believe by Lauren D. Woods, winner of the 2024 Fiction Prize, selected by Kristen Arnett

Self-Portrait as the "i" in Florida by P. Scott Cunningham, winner of the 2025 Donald Justice Poetry Prize, selected by Major Jackson

Les Portes by Meredith Nnoka, winner of the 2025 CAAPP Book Prize, selected by Cameron Awkward-Rich

Magdalena Is Brighter Than You Think by Grace Spulak, winner of the 2025 Rising Writer Prize, selected by K-Ming Chang